The Salem Witch Trials

Other titles in the American History series

The American Revolution
The Constitution and Founding of America
Twentieth-Century Immigration to the United States

AMERICAN HISTORY

The Salem Witch Trials

Don Nardo

LUCENT BOOKS
An imprint of Thomson Gale, a part of The Thomson Corporation

THOMSON
™
GALE

Detroit • New York • San Francisco • New Haven, Conn. • Waterville, Maine • London

© 2007 Thomson Gale, a part of The Thomson Corporation.

Thomson and Star Logo are trademarks and Gale and Lucent Books are registered trademarks used herein under license.

For more information, contact
Lucent Books
27500 Drake Rd.
Farmington Hills, MI 48331-3535
Or you can visit our Internet site at http://www.gale.com

LIBRARY OF CONGRESS CATALOGING-IN-PUBLICATION DATA

Nardo, Don, 1947-
   The Salem witch trials / by Don Nardo.
      p. cm. — (American history)
   Includes bibliographical references and index.
   ISBN-13: 978-1-59018-950-4 (hardcover)
   1. Trials (Witchcraft)—Massachusetts—Salem—History—17th century—
Juvenile literature. 2. Witchcraft—Massachusetts—Salem—History—
17th century—Juvenile literature. I. Title.
   KFM2478.8.W5N37 2007
   133.4'3097445—dc22
                                                          2007006847

ISBN-10: 1-59018-950-7

Printed in the United States of America

Contents

Foreword

The United States has existed as a nation for just over 200 years. By comparison, Rome existed as a nation-state for more than 1000 years. Out of a few struggling British colonies, the United States developed relatively quickly into a world power whose policy decisions and culture have great influence on the world stage. What events and aspirations drove this young American nation to such great heights in such a short period of time? The answer lies in a close study of its varied and unique history. As James Baldwin once remarked, "American history is longer, larger, more various, more beautiful, and more terrible than anything anyone has ever said about it."

The basic facts of United States history—names, dates, places, battles, treaties, speeches, and acts of Congress—fill countless textbooks. These facts, though essential to a thorough understanding of world events, are rarely compelling for students. More compelling are the stories in history, the experience of history.

Titles in this series explore the history of the country and the experiences of Americans. What influences led the colonists to risk everything and break from Britain? Who was the driving force behind the Constitution? Which factors led thousands of people to leave their homelands and settle in the United States? Questions like these do not have simple answers; by discussing them, however, we can view the past as a more real, interesting, and accessible place.

Students will find excellent tools for research and investigation in every title. Lucent Books' American History series provides not only facts, but also the analysis and context necessary for insightful critical thinking about history and about current events. Fully cited quotations from historical figures, eyewitnesses, letters, speeches, and writings bring vibrancy and authority to the text. Annotated bibliographies allow students to evaluate and locate sources for further investigation. Sidebars highlight important and interesting figures, events, or related primary source excerpts. Timelines, maps, and full color images add another dimension of accessibility to the stories being told.

It has been said the past has a history of repeating itself, for good and ill. In these pages, students will learn a bit about both and, perhaps, better understand their own place in this world.

1233
Pope Gregory IX establishes the medieval Inquisition, which eventually hunts down witches.

1347
The bubonic plague, or Black Death, strikes large portions of Europe.

1431
The Inquisition arrests, tries, and executes the French warrior-maiden Joan of Arc for witchcraft.

1200	1300	1400	1500

1484
Pope Innocent VIII declares in an edict that witches are real.

1492
Sailing for Spain, Italian-born mariner Christopher Columbus lands in the West Indies, initiating a great age of global exploration.

1530s
English king Henry VIII separates his nation from Roman Catholicism, creating the Protestant Church of England.

of the Salem Witch Trials

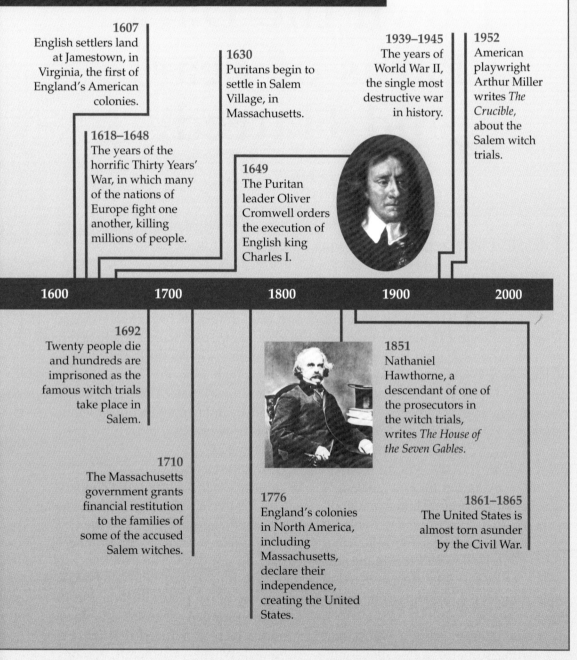

1607
English settlers land at Jamestown, in Virginia, the first of England's American colonies.

1630
Puritans begin to settle in Salem Village, in Massachusetts.

1939–1945
The years of World War II, the single most destructive war in history.

1952
American playwright Arthur Miller writes *The Crucible*, about the Salem witch trials.

1618–1648
The years of the horrific Thirty Years' War, in which many of the nations of Europe fight one another, killing millions of people.

1649
The Puritan leader Oliver Cromwell orders the execution of English king Charles I.

1600   **1700**   **1800**   **1900**   **2000**

1692
Twenty people die and hundreds are imprisoned as the famous witch trials take place in Salem.

1851
Nathaniel Hawthorne, a descendant of one of the prosecutors in the witch trials, writes *The House of the Seven Gables*.

1710
The Massachusetts government grants financial restitution to the families of some of the accused Salem witches.

1776
England's colonies in North America, including Massachusetts, declare their independence, creating the United States.

1861–1865
The United States is almost torn asunder by the Civil War.

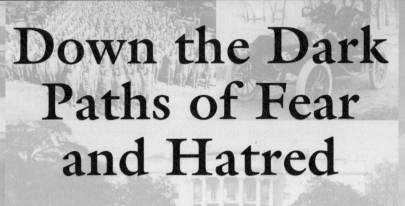

Down the Dark Paths of Fear and Hatred

Imagine a situation in which the daughter of a neighbor, a young woman who has never before exhibited odd behavior, suddenly begins acting strangely. She repeatedly falls onto the ground and has seizure-like fits. Hearing about it, the local authorities arrive and examine the girl. But instead of diagnosing her outbursts as symptoms of a medical condition, the leaders of the community declare that her fits are being caused by witches, who are tormenting her and trying to get her to worship the devil. Moreover, the young woman begins accusing her own neighbors of secretly being witches. Though no tangible proof exists to support these accusations, the authorities readily believe her and begin arresting and trying the suspects. One by one they are convicted of committing evil deeds and suffer execution by hanging.

At first glance, such a weird and frightening scenario seems like something out of a grisly old European fairy tale or a bad horror movie. Yet the sad truth is that it actually happened in Salem, Massachusetts, in the 1690s. Several young women began having fits, and the authorities became convinced that they were the victims of witchcraft. Large numbers of people in the community were then accused of being witches, tried, and convicted; of these, hundreds were jailed, and twenty, including a minister and several frail elderly women, were executed.

How could such a travesty of justice have occurred in a supposedly civilized society? After all, witches—when defined as followers of Satan who use evil, supernatural powers to do his bidding—clearly do not exist. The problem was that at the time of the Salem witch trials, a majority of people in Europe and its recently founded colonies in North America were convinced that witches were real. Witches, witchcraft, demons, sorcery, and other supernatural beings and practices were part of the accepted religious and social world view of the times. The arrest, prosecution, imprisonment, and execution of suspected witches in Salem were, therefore, the result of widespread ignorance, superstition, and fear. These factors combined to produce one of the most disturbing and best documented cases of mass hysteria in history. (Mass hysteria occurs when the members of a group all become convinced that something with no basis in fact is actually real.)

Roots of the Fear of Witches

The sordid and tragic events of the trials in Salem are, historically speaking, noteworthy in their own right. Indeed, they constitute one of the most extreme, fas-

cinating, and often-written-about incidents in American history. But this localized outbreak of contagious fear and violence is also important because it sheds light on other similar cases of mass hysteria, persecution, and grave injustice in the human saga. In the words of Frances Hill, one of the leading modern scholars of the Salem witch trials, these troubling incidents

provide an astonishingly clear and instructive model of the universal and timeless processes by which groups of human beings instigate, justify, and escalate persecution. . . . Because the numbers of people involved in the Salem witch-hunt and the time-scale of events were on a small scale, the steps are easy

In this sixteenth-century illustration, three accused witches are burned alive.

To the residents of Salem, Massachusetts, in 1692, this tree was thought to be a gathering spot for witches to perform their rituals.

Those dark paths had formed long before as a set of fear-based religious and social beliefs about witches. And a brief examination of these beliefs reveals the roots of the strange, twisted mindset that gripped those who sought out and killed witches in Salem in the late 1600s.

At that time, Europe had only recently emerged from its medieval era (roughly spanning the years 500 to 1600), and a number of common folk beliefs and myths of that period were still widely accepted, including those relating to witches. In medieval times in Europe, witches were usually seen as women, but also sometimes men, who did the bidding of the devil. It was thought that witches engaged in sexual acts with the devil or with demons; flew through the sky; turned themselves into wolves, bats, and other animals; became invisible at will; and harassed or corrupted average people.

The *Witches' Hammer*

Although people all over Europe readily believed in witches, for several centuries these supernatural beings were viewed as a relatively minor threat to society. Even when Pope Gregory IX authorized the killing of witches in the 1200s, few were hunted down and exe-

to trace, by which a few deranged, destructive human beings led ordinary mortals down the dark paths of fear, hatred, and envy to demonize and destroy innocent victims. When those steps are understood, the recurrent persecutions in human history, whether, ethnic, religious, political, or superstitious, become less hard to comprehend.[1]

In fact, the "dark paths of fear and hatred" that caused the persecution of suspected witches in Salem were by no means new to the inhabitants of Massachusetts and their European forebears.

cuted in the two centuries that followed. The situation changed, however, and much for the worse, after another pope, Innocent VIII, released an edict in 1484. It stated in no uncertain terms that witches were real. Because the Church then held sway over the minds of most Europeans, large numbers of people took the pope's words quite seriously. And those few who doubted that witches were real were silenced by the fear of being branded a heretic (someone who, in thought or deed, goes against the teachings of God and the Church).

To reinforce Pope Innocent's tough stance against witches, in 1486 two German Dominican monks, James Sprenger and Heinrich Kramer, published the *Malleus Maleficarum*, or *Witches' Hammer*. This volume listed the supernatural acts performed by witches and told how witches caused disease, destroyed crops, and kidnapped and ate innocent children. At the time, monks were among the few educated people in Europe. And people tended to assume that a book written by monks and approved by the pope must be both righteous and factual. Not surprisingly, considering the cultural backwardness of the times, no one seemed to notice the authors' narrow-mindedness, vitriolic hatred of women, sick sexual obsessions, and lack of sympathy for normal human feelings. Typical is the following passage, in which the monks explain why witches are more apt to be female than male:

> Now the wickedness of women is spoken of in [the Bible, which says that] . . . all wickedness is but little

to the wickedness of a woman. . . . What else is woman but a foe to friendship, an unescapable punishment, a necessary evil, a natural temptation, a desirable calamity, a domestic danger, a delectable detriment, an evil of nature, painted with fair colors! . . . The many lusts of men lead them into one sin, but the lust of women leads them into all sins; for the root of all woman's

Hysteria against witches grew considerably in 1484, when Pope Innocent VIII stated that witches were real.

In 1486, James Sprenger and Heinrich Kramer published the Malleus Maleficarum, *or* Witches' Hammer, *a book about the supernatural acts performed by witches.*

vices is avarice [greed]. . . . [Holy writings contain some descriptions of good, religiously devout women, but in many other passages] the word *woman* is used to mean the lust of the flesh. As it is said: I have found a woman more bitter than death, and a good woman subject to carnal lust. Other reasons why there are more superstitious women found than men . . . women are nat-

urally more impressionable, and more ready to receive the influence of a disembodied spirit . . . they have slippery tongues, and are unable to conceal from their fellow-women those things which by evil arts they know; and, since they are weak, they find an easy and secret manner of vindicating themselves by witchcraft. . . . We may add . . . that since they are feebler both in mind and body, it is not surprising that they should come more under the spell of witchcraft.[2]

A Holocaust of Witches

Thanks to Sprenger and Kramer's book, sermons based on it, and other church-sanctioned ravings about witches, a wave of mass hysteria about the threat of witches began to sweep over Europe. In the two centuries that followed, hunts, trials, and executions of witches occurred in Germany, Italy, France, Sweden, Switzerland, Spain, and other lands. "Most of the victims," says James A. Haught, a scholar who specializes in the history of religious persecutions,

were old women whose [stooped posture, wrinkled skin, and seemingly odd personal habits] roused the suspicions of neighbors. Others were young, pretty women. Some were men. Many in continental Europe were simply citizens whose names were shrieked out by torture victims when commanded to identify fellow witches.[3]

In fact, torture was a regular feature of the persecution and prosecution of suspected witches. The authorities inflicted gruesome physical abuses on the victims, in part to get them to confess to practicing witchcraft, and also to divulge the names of other witches. Usually, the suspects were stripped of their clothes. Then their hair was shaved and often their fingernails were yanked out. It was common to apply red-hot metal tongs to the victim's breasts and genitals and to stretch the person's body on a rack, dislocating many of the joints. The results of these cruelties were predictable; as Haught puts it, "Virtually every mangled and broken victim confessed—and was executed on the basis of the confession."[4]

The total number of European women and sometimes men who were tortured and killed on suspicion of being witches is unknown. Estimates by modern scholars range from about one hundred thousand to as many as 2 million. Eventually, this virtual holocaust of witches ran its course.

Arrests of suspected witches had dramatically declined in number by the late 1600s and early 1700s, partly because of the more rational thinking that attended the rise of modern science in those years.

Thus, the Salem witch trials, which took place in a European outpost, represented one of the last gasps of the witch mania that had so long infected Europe. Though they happened far across the sea from the sites of the medieval witch hunts, the shameful incidents in Salem were in a number of ways linked to those earlier travesties of justice. The Salem witch trials "could never have happened," Hill points out, "if the supernatural beliefs the Puritans had brought with them from England . . . had not retained their conviction and power right through the seventeenth century."[5] Only after the slaughter of innocents in Salem had finally abated did the force of reason begin to illuminate the darkness of fear and superstition that had so long pervaded the human spirit.

Chapter One

Salem on the Eve of the Witch Trials

Looking back on the Salem witch trials from a modern vantage, it is clear that they would not have displayed the same rabid intensity and grim outcome had they occurred in another place and time. Indeed, the particular physical and cultural setting of seventeenth-century Salem made the witch hunt, trials, and executions possible. Especially important in this regard were the unique beliefs and customs of the Puritans who then lived in Salem and other nearby towns. They led spare, simplistic lives devoid of material luxury and excess, and individuality of any kind was discouraged. In a society that featured a lot of drudgery and monotony, emphasized sameness, and condoned only a narrow set of behaviors, any unusual behavior was bound to cause a stir.

Especially noteworthy were behaviors that deviated from the norms of Puritan religious life. The Puritans were extremely devout fundamentalist Christians who

felt that God was watching them closely and would punish them for even minor sins and antisocial acts. Puritan ministers and elders heavily emphasized the ongoing battle between God and the devil and warned that Satan's helpers, including witches, were both real and a constant danger to all members of the community. Only in such an atmosphere could there be such ready acceptance of the notion that many of one's neighbors were secretly witches. People "noticed their neighbors' misfortunes," scholar Marilynne K. Roach points out,

> [such as] a lame horse or a dead child, and wondered if this were God's punishment. With good and evil so obviously present in the world, to question the devil's reality was to doubt God's. Few doubted. Since there was a devil, it followed that some wicked or foolish mortals would pay allegiance to

The Puritans were extremely devout fundamentalist Christians.

him in return for . . . the power to work evil magic. . . . Therefore, contemporary scholars argued, devils performed the magic for the witches, who either consciously collaborated or were deluded into thinking they did it themselves.[6]

Thus, to understand how seventeenth-century Salem was consumed by a disastrous witch hunt, one must first examine the town, its habitants, their background, and their peculiar beliefs and customs on the eve of the infamous witch trials.

Emergence of the Puritans and Their Colonies

The religious sect that came to be known as Puritanism emerged from the turmoil surrounding the early years of the Church of England. Before the sixteenth century, England, like other European lands, was a Catholic country that, in religious matters, recognized the authority of the pope in Rome. That situation changed quite suddenly and drastically in the 1530s. When the religious authorities in Rome refused to grant the English king, Henry VIII, a divorce, he angrily and boldly separated his country from the established church. The result was the formation of the Church of England, a Protestant denomination of Christianity.

As time went on, the English monarchs and most of their subjects felt that their new church satisfactorily met their needs. However, a few of the more devout inhabitants of the country were not so happy with the new religious climate. They came to view the new church as too liberal and permissive, even as corrupt. Because they desired to purify the church by taking it back to stricter, more fundamental Christian ideas and customs, they became known as Puritans.

It is perhaps not surprising that the Puritans quickly earned a reputation as troublemakers, especially to the reigning monarchs and high-ranking churchmen. And in the early 1600s, these leaders began to persecute the Puritans. In

Henry VIII broke away from the Catholic Church and formed the Church of England in the 1530s.

A God-Fearing People

The extreme degree of piety felt and displayed by the vast majority of colonial Puritans is part-ly revealed by the words of a sermon delivered by the early Puritan minister and governor John Winthrop in 1630:

The eyes of all people are upon us, so that if we shall deal falsely with our God in this work we have undertaken and to cause him to withdraw his present help from us, we shall be made a story . . . through the world, we shall open the mouths of enemies to speak evil of the ways of God. . . . There is now set before us life, and good, death, and evil in that we are commanded this day to love the Lord our God, and to love one another, to walk in his ways and to keep his commandments . . . and his laws. . . . But if our hearts shall turn away [from God] so that we will not obey [him], we shall surely perish.

Quoted in The Religious Freedom Page, "A Model of Christian Charity." http://religiousfreedom.lib.virginia.edu/sacred/charity.html.

response, some of the latter fled to Holland, while one group of Puritans crossed the Atlantic in 1620 and established a colony at Plymouth, in what is now southern Massachusetts. The Plymouth Puritans came to be known as the Pilgrims.

Not long after the landfall at Plymouth, other Puritans arrived and settled in an area further north on the Massachusetts coast. In 1628, a Puritan leader named John Endecott came with about fifty followers and founded Salem, which grew into the first town in a large new colony—Massachusetts Bay. Other Puritans were soon drawn to this new North American outpost. John Winthrop,

who became the first governor of the colony, led about a thousand of them to Salem in 1630. But because of overcrowding, many of these newcomers struck out on their own and established new towns nearby, including Watertown, Medford, and Dorchester. The largest group of Puritans settled along the Charles River about fifteen miles (24km) south of Salem at a spot they named Boston. Boston grew rapidly, taking in almost ten thousand more Puritan immigrants by 1640.

Salem Town and Salem Village

Also established in the Massachusetts Bay Colony during this period was Salem

John Winthrop, the first governor of Massachusetts, comes ashore at Salem in 1630.

Village, at first called Salem Farms. Salem Village was a separate entity from Salem Town. Lying along the coast, Salem Town was a bustling port with a number of shops, large merchants' houses, and local government buildings. In contrast, Salem Village (which is now the small town of Danvers) consisted of a few scattered farms and farmhouses roughly clustered around the village center. That center eventually featured a meetinghouse, which doubled as a church, a parsonage (home for the local minister), a small tavern, and a few houses owned by local tradesmen. Beyond the

village's cultivated fields stretched large expanses of uncharted forests inhabited only by Indian tribes.

The remoteness of Salem Village from the other Puritan towns is illustrated by the fact that it took a person two to three hours to walk from the village to Salem Town. The distance between them was only about five miles (8km), but travelers had to cross several small rivers and inlets. At first, this arduous trip presented a major physical challenge to the residents of Salem Village. Before the meetinghouse was erected in the village center in 1672, every Sunday they had to walk all the way to the church in Salem Town and back again.

This initial reliance on the church and other facilities in the town was not the only source of frustration to the inhabitants of Salem Village. For a long time, they had little say in running their village, which fell under the legal and political jurisdiction of Salem Town. The leaders of the town taxed the villagers and set the prices for crops and other items exported from the village to the town. The town's elders also appointed the village's constable and controlled the distribution of land parcels and the building of roads in the village. For years, village leaders repeatedly lodged complaints and petitions in an effort to gain more autonomy. But it was not until 1752, long after the Salem witch trials had ended, that the village finally broke free and became the independent town of Danvers.

Contempt for Luxury and Open Discrimination

Even when the citizens of Salem Village got their own meetinghouse in 1672, no one viewed it as a luxury, partly because the Puritan ethic rejected the very idea of luxury or any form of personal pleasure. In fact, Puritan society vigorously promoted a spartan existence, even

when worshipping God. Like other Puritan meetinghouses, the one in Salem Village had no heat. Worshippers were allowed to bring blankets, but on the harshest winter days these provided only minimal relief from the numbing cold. The summer, in contrast, brought a different sort of discomfort in the form of

The interior of a Puritan meetinghouse is very plain in appearance to comply with Puritan ideals.

mosquitoes, flies, and ticks from a near-by swamp.

One could not avoid these uncomfortable, unhealthy conditions simply by choosing to stay home on Sunday. In Salem, as in other Puritan communities, attending church was mandated by law. Everyone, without exception, had to sit through a three-hour service on Sunday morning and a two-hour service on Sunday afternoon. The rest of the day was devoted to prayer, Bible reading, and other religious activities. Moreover, during the formal services the worshippers were literally forced to pay attention to the minister; an individual called a tithing man walked through the aisles and used his hand or a stick to prod any-

Puritan society was very strict. Those who did not closely follow the rules were dealt with harshly.

one who fell asleep or tried to whisper something to his or her neighbor.

The strictness of Puritan laws and customs relating to religious worship was matched by the harsh manner in which society treated many of its members. The Puritans openly practiced what today are recognized as serious forms of discrimination and abuse. In general, society catered to the young, the strong, the wealthy, and the male. Women were seen as inferior, as were poor people, most elderly persons (especially old women), and handicapped people; of the latter, those born with severe birth defects were viewed as the devil's offspring. (The notion that women, particularly old ones, were the most likely members of society to be witches was inherent in this social prejudice, a bias the Puritans inherited from the recent witch hunts in Europe.)

Gender and class discrimination even invaded the church, where the wealthiest people got the best seats (in front, closest to the pulpit) and men and women sat in separate sections. Puritan teachings and ministers claimed that such social divisions and unequal treatment were God's will. And with only very rare exceptions, no one dared to question this view.

Trying Not to Anger God

These attitudes and practices show how thoroughly God and religious ideas and observances pervaded Salem and other Puritan enclaves in the Massachusetts Bay Colony. Indeed, God's will, good versus evil, and divine punishment were concepts that regularly spilled over from the church into all areas of society and human endeavor. The common belief was that nearly everything people did and said was somehow connected to God and had divine consequences of some kind. As historian Richard Weisman explains:

> Crop failures, epidemics, Indian raids, and sundry other disasters were perceived not as accidents or as the mere logical [aspects] of wilderness living, but rather as judgments rendered according to the moral failings of the community. As the national sins increased, so would the severity of divine afflictions. Insofar as God maintained his covenant with [Puritan society in] New England, the members would have clear and continuous guidelines regarding the extent of their progress toward or departure from the realization of communal goals.[7]

If the community was to thrive, therefore, people must be careful not to provoke or anger God in any way, no matter how slight. This is part of the reason that the Puritans banned all forms of public entertainment, including dancing and going to the theater. They viewed such activities as frivolous, against God's will, and inspired by the devil. Even when worshippers sang hymns in church, they did so in a droning monotone, believing that the expression of a catchy tune might bring the singers pleasure; and in their view, God frowned on all forms of

pleasure. Living under the constraints of such a stern and authoritarian mindset, it was easy to conclude that anyone who veered from these rules was potentially an agent of the devil.

It was not only personal enjoyment that supposedly kindled God's displeasure in Salem and other Puritan towns. Any sort of rule breaking or social nonconformity was seen as a threat to society, and the perpetrator was subject to public punishment. Among the common sins and crimes were failing to attend church; engaging in any sexual act, even a mere kiss, in public; breaking an engagement to be married; and disagreeing with community leaders on any matter. One common punishment was to be tied to a post and whipped. Another was to sit for hours or days in the stocks, wooden frameworks that trapped a person's hands, feet, and/or head. Still another penalty was exile, as happened to a Salemite named Roger Williams; his offense was to

In Puritan society any social nonconformity was seen as a threat, and the perpetrator was subject to public punishment.

promote the idea that people should be allowed to worship how and when they pleased. In 1635, he was banished and soon afterward established a new colony farther south, in what is now Rhode Island. The harshest punishment meted out in the Massachusetts Bay Colony was death, usually by hanging. This is how nineteen of the twenty accused witches who were condemned to be executed in Salem met their untimely end.

Pent-up Passions Pour Out

The Puritans' strict religious beliefs, customs, laws, and punishments were not the only factors that were destined to contribute to the wholesale prosecution of witches in Salem. True, an unhealthy preoccupation with the devil and the ongoing struggle between the forces of good and evil made many of the town's inhabitants believe that witches might actually be living among them. But no one would have been accused of witchcraft in the first place if it had not been for the strange behavior of a few local young people. They succeeded in making nearly everyone in their society believe that they had been tormented and possessed by witches. Their personal fascination with the supernatural and the attention and notoriety they received when they underwent violent physical convulsions were key factors in the witch hysteria that gripped the town.

In this regard, the fact that all of these young people were female is revealing. In Puritan society in general, and especially in the small, remote village of Salem, women had far fewer opportuni-ties and outlets for personal expression and satisfaction than men had. In winter, scholar Marion L. Starkey writes, men were relieved of most of their more time-consuming farm chores and

> they could take a musket into the forest to shoot wild turkey, deer, and a marauding fox or wolf. Or they could fetch a line and hook, cut through the ice, and fish. House-bound, they could turn to the secondary trade that nearly every Puritan frontiersman practiced in his spare time. Some cobbled shoes. Some fashioned trays . . . of good-smelling wood. . . . Men and boys were not often idle, not often bored.[8]

By contrast, women in Salem Village, especially younger women, led lives that can only be described as subservient, narrow, smotheringly restrictive, and monotonous in the extreme. They were far from idle; indeed, they regularly did housework and farm chores. But for them, life was, for all intents and purposes, nothing but work—work of a very repetitious nature with little or no element of novelty, creativity, or enjoyment. "For young girls still unspoken-for," Starkey points out, "winter was unrelieved drudgery."[9]

Furthermore, young people in Puritan Salem had no outlet for the enthusiasm, curiosity, and awakening sexual urges that are normal for young men and women. Today, people often speak of young people rebelling against their elders, a behavior that is expected and considered normal,

A Wide Range of Offenses

Like the Puritans' religious beliefs and practices, their legal system was extremely strict and harsh, recognizing a wide range of criminal offenses. Most of these are today viewed as mere personal foibles or even as normal behavior. Among the many cases that came to court in Salem on a single day, June 27, 1664, were the following:

Robert Goodell [is to be] fined for suffering his goat to go in his neighbor's cornfield. Alice George of Gloucester [is] to be whipped or fined for railing against [scolding] Mr. Blynman, calling him [a] "wicked wretch.". . . Michael Lambert of Lynn [got] drunk. [He later] confessed that he had drunk three or four cups of sack [liquor]. . . . John Stone of Gloucester [will be] fined for scandalizing [saying derogatory things behind the back of] Mr. Blynman. . . . Alice Williams [is to be] fined five pounds and whipped for fornication [having sex] with William Flynt. . . . James George, servant to William Cantleburie, [is] to be whipped for running away from his master.

Quoted in Frances Hill, ed., *The Salem Witch Trials Reader*. New York: Da Capo, 2000, pp. 35–36.

even healthy. But young Puritans, particularly young women, had no socially accepted way to rebel. So they channeled their repressed natural feelings into other areas, particularly into excessive, overly dramatic displays of religious zeal. These might include swooning or fainting during Bible readings or sermons that described the sufferings of Jesus Christ or repeating the same prayer over and over again for hours on end.

Either Saints or Devils

Eventually, several young women in Salem Village took such displays to a new level. They allowed their pent-up feelings and energies to pour out in the performance of seizure-like fits supposedly caused by the assaults of witches. Along with these turbulent episodes, the girls received a sort of twisted gratification from the excitement of the witch trials they helped to bring about. In a way, says Carol F. Karlsen, a historian at the University of Michigan, they thereby became the central figures in a "social drama" in which

the more attention they received, the more they dramatized their socially generated anguish and their internally generated desire to rebel. As the community looked on, their bodies expressed what they otherwise could not: that the enormous pressures put upon them to accept a religiously based, male-centered social order was more than they could bear. To accept the community's truth was to deny the self. . . . Their religious beliefs led the possessed finally to confirm the only reality their culture allowed, the reality articulated by their ministers. . . . There were only two kinds of women: godly women and witches.[10]

This stark contrast between good and evil, with no allowance for any gray area in between, was typical for Puritan society on the eve of the famous witch trials. The residents of Salem Village, along with the residents of neighboring towns, had long been led to believe, by both their ministers and elders, that there were only two kinds of people. In the words of the Reverend Samuel Parris, who came to play a key role in the trials, one was either a "saint," meaning a good, god-fearing person, or a "devil," a damnable sinner or witch. In a sermon delivered in March 1692, Parris declared:

Christ knows who these devils are [in our church]. . . . Christ knows how many devils [walk] among us—whether one, or ten, or twenty. And also who they are. He knows us perfectly. And he knows those of us who are in his church, that we are either saints or devils, true believers, or hypocrites and dissembling Judases who would sell Christ and his kingdom to gratify [their sinful] lust.[11]

In a society so fear-ridden and brainwashed that its members could listen to and readily believe these paranoid words, it would take only a tiny spark of suspicion to ignite a blaze of terror, hysteria, and injustice. And that is exactly what happened in Salem Village beginning early in 1692.

Chapter Two

Strange Behaviors Diagnosed as Witchcraft

The outbreak of witchcraft hysteria in colonial Salem Village began on a February day in 1692. Two young girls, Elizabeth Parris and Abigail Williams, began having strange, at times frightening, fits, which filled their elders with concern. It was not long before the leaders of the community diagnosed the cause of this unusual behavior as witchcraft. In their view, the violent fits could not be the result of the girls' own physical or mental processes; rather, there had to be some nefarious outside influence that had taken hold of the poor girls—namely witches, pernicious agents of the devil.

Most people today would not jump to the outlandish conclusion that a person suffering from physical convulsions must be possessed or harassed by evil beings. Why did Salem's leaders rush to that judgment? In part, their ready willingness to blame witchcraft stemmed from some related events that had

occurred not long before in colonial New England. In 1656, 1662, and again in 1689, only three years before the start of the Salem witch trials, women in Puritan communities had been prosecuted and executed for practicing witchcraft.

These earlier trials, which are seldom talked about today, set an important precedent in Puritan society. When Elizabeth Parris and Abigail Williams began having fits, Puritan elders, including Cotton Mather, minister of Boston's North Church (not to be confused with that city's Old North Church), were reminded of the events and victims of the earlier witch trials. Thus, the initial sparks that ignited the trials in Salem, like the trials themselves, did not emerge from a vacuum. They were part of an unhealthy, potentially dangerous social and psychological atmosphere that had long pervaded the Puritan communities.

The Initial Puritan Witch Trials

Among the prior witch hunts that Mather and other commentators of the Salem trials remembered was the earliest recorded arrest and execution of a colonial Puritan for witchcraft. Anne Hibbins, of Boston, was the sister of a colonial governor, Richard Bellingham, and the wife of a prominent merchant, William Hibbins. Unfortunately for Mrs. Hibbins, she earned a reputation for having a temper and speaking her mind, traits unbecoming women in Puritan society. In particular, she was chastised on several occasions for raising her voice to and arguing with men.

Not long after her husband died in 1654, Anne Hibbins saw two men conversing in the street, and though they were beyond earshot, she deduced they were talking about her. When she mentioned this observation to some neighbors, they reported her to the authorities. The latter promptly arrested her, claiming that the only way she could have known she was the subject of the men's conversation was to exercise evil powers, specifically the supernatural abilities attributed to witches. A jury found her guilty and she was executed in 1656.

Another witch trial and execution occurred in Hartford, now the chief city of the state of Connecticut, six years later. (Hartford had been founded in 1636 by a small group of Massachusetts Puritans.) It is important to note that the supposed victim of witchcraft in this case, Anne Cole, exhibited many of the same physical symptoms—including convulsions—later displayed by Elizabeth Parris and Abigail Williams in Salem. About Cole's disturbing symptoms, Increase Mather, a prominent Puritan minister and Cotton Mather's father, wrote:

> She was and is accounted a person of real piety and integrity. Nevertheless, in the Year 1662 . . . she was taken with very strange fits, wherein her tongue was [caused] by a demon to express things which she herself knew nothing of. Sometimes the [evil ravings] would hold [go on] for a considerable time.[12]

It did not take the local authorities long to arrest another Hartford woman, Rebecca Greensmith, and charge her with using evil powers to afflict poor Anne Cole. For reasons unknown, Greensmith confessed to being a witch. Perhaps she was tortured and to avoid further agony said whatever her tormentors wanted her to. In any case, Increase Mather reported that she described how

> the Devil first appeared to her in the form of a deer or fawn, skipping about her, wherewith she was not much afraid, and that by degrees he became very familiar, and at last would talk with her. Moreover, she said that the Devil had frequently [had] the carnal knowledge of her body. And that the witches had meetings at a place not far from her house; and that some appeared in one shape, and others in another; and one came flying amongst them in the shape of a crow.[13]

Sufferings of the Goodwin Children

In his Memorable Providences, *penned in 1689, the Reverend Cotton Mather recalled the physical symptoms reportedly suffered by four of John Goodwin's children in Boston the year before:*

Sometimes they would be deaf, sometimes dumb, and sometimes blind, and often, all this at once. One time, their tongues would be drawn down their throats; another time, they would be pulled out on their chins, to a prodigious [great] length. They would have their mouths opened unto such a wideness that their jaws went out of joint. . . . The same would happen to their shoulder-blades, and their elbows, and hand-wrists, and several of the joints. They would at times lie in a benumbed condition. . . . They would make most piteous outcries, [saying] that they were cut with knives and struck with blows that they could not bear. Their necks would be broken, so that their neck-bone would seem dissolved . . . yea, their heads would be twisted almost around.

Quoted in Frances Hill, ed., *The Salem Witch Trials Reader.* New York: Da Capo, 2000, p. 19.

Based on this confession, Rebecca Greensmith was executed, along with her husband, whom the authorities concluded had helped her commit evil deeds.

Another case in which Puritan children suffered fits very similar to those of Elizabeth Parris and Abigail Williams took place in Boston in 1688. Four of the six offspring of a reputable mason named John Goodwin were affected, as later told by Cotton Mather:

The children were tormented just in the same part of their bodies all at the same time together. . . . Likewise, their pains and sprains were swift like lightning, yet when the neck, or the hand, or the back of one was racked, so it was at that instant with the others, too. . . . Sometimes they would be deaf, sometimes dumb, and sometimes blind. . . . Their tongues would be drawn down their throats . . . [and] their heads would be twisted almost around.[14]

The children blamed an Irish Catholic laundress, Goodwife Glover, for their strange afflictions. ("Goodwife," sometimes shortened to "Goody," and "Goodman," were titles commonly given to working-class Puritans.) The authorities, who already viewed Mrs. Glover with suspicion because she was Catholic, agreed that she was the culprit. They tried her as a witch and hanged her.

Tituba's Secret Circle

There was, therefore, ample precedent in New England's Puritan communities for young people having physical convulsions and blaming them on supposed witches. Moreover, it is likely no coincidence that the first children to suffer such fits in Salem lived in the house of the local minister. Reverend Samuel Parris had moved to Salem from Boston in 1689, only about a year after the execution of Goodwife Glover. Parris and the members of his family—including his wife, three children, and niece, Abigail Williams—were surely well acquainted with Glover's trial and the debilitating physical symptoms supposedly suffered by John Goodwin's children. The fact that nine-year-old Elizabeth Parris, nicknamed "Betty," and eleven-year-old Abigail knew about the Goodwin children and might have copied their symptoms, either consciously or unconsciously, is often overlooked in modern studies of the Salem witch trials.

Another factor that made the Parris household a likely place for strange and seemingly supernatural behaviors to occur was the presence of two Caribbean Indians. When they moved from Boston to Salem, the Parris family brought along two slaves native to Barbados—John Indian and his wife, Tituba. (Owning slaves was very uncommon in the colonies at the time; only about three or four hundred African and Indian slaves then existed in all of New England.) John worked in the fields and tended the family's livestock. Tituba cleaned the house and did laundry and other chores. She also cared for and entertained the Parris children on a regular basis because Mrs. Parris was often sick and unable to perform these motherly duties.

Like other young Puritan girls, Betty and Abigail were often bored, particularly in the winter months, and welcomed the attentions of Tituba, clearly an offbeat character in Puritan society. The girls frequently spent hours at a time listening to the older woman tell stories about her native land. It was only natural for Tituba to include information about magic in these sessions, since both black and white magic were features of Caribbean island culture. (Black magic consisted of spells intended to hurt other people; white magic was thought to bring good fortune or to reveal glimpses of the future.) Thus, the presence of Tituba in the household almost ensured that the Parris children would be exposed to knowledge of the supernatural.

The exact sequence of events leading from Betty and Abigail's listening to stories and playing games with Tituba to the girls' first experiences with seizure-like fits is unclear. What seems certain is that at some point in the winter of 1692 Tituba and the girls played a game that supposedly could reveal certain future events. Specifically, it was thought to predict the professions of the girls' future husbands. One played the game by dropping an egg white into a glass of water. If the egg white formed a shape that looked like a hammer, it indicated that the future husband would be a carpenter. Various other shapes stood for other professions.

Tituba weaves stories about magic for the children of the household.

Playing such a game today would likely be seen as harmless fun. But in seventeenth-century Puritan society, such games were forbidden because magic was thought to be the devil's work. Thus, Betty and Abigail were aware that what they were doing was wrong in the eyes of their parents and society, yet as children with natural urges to experiment and rebel, they did it anyway. In fact, they told some of their closer friends about their secret games, and Tituba's circle of young followers widened. One of the first outsiders to join was twelve-year-old Ann Putnam, daughter of Thomas Putnam, a local farmer whose

family owned a lot of land and wielded much social influence in Salem. Next came Mary Walcott, sixteen, whose father's farm bordered the two-acre parsonage on which the Parris family lived. Seventeen-year-old Elizabeth Hubbard, the great-niece of the local doctor, William Griggs, also joined Tituba's circle, as did Susan Sheldon, Elizabeth Booth, Mercy Lewis, and Mary Warren, all in their late teens.

Each member of this covert group was sworn to secrecy. Clearly, none wished to be punished, which was sure to happen if their parents found out. But the children did not then appreciate an important fact of life and human nature, namely that the more people who know a secret, the more likely it is that the secret will be revealed. They were also unprepared for their hidden games to take a serious and frightening turn, which they did. One day when they dropped an egg white into some water it formed a shape that to Tituba and the girls looked like a coffin, then as now a symbol of death and ill fortune. This proved to be the fateful turning point for the girls and for their community. From that day forward, the girls began to exhibit the convulsions and other disturbing physical behaviors that would lead to the famous witch trials.

Physical Manifestations of Fear?

In retrospect, it is difficult to know specifically which fears drove Betty, Abigail, and the other girls to display these weird behaviors. Some of the girls may have interpreted the coffin-shaped egg white as a sign that they would have bleak futures. It is also possible that some or all of them viewed the death symbol as a sign from God, admonishing them for playing forbidden games. But probably more of the girls' growing trepidation was caused by fear and guilt already programmed into them by the society in which they lived. On the one hand, there was guilt over having flirted with evil forces, which might well land them in hell; on the other hand, there was surely a lurking fear that their elders would find out what they had been doing and subject them to terrible punishments, perhaps even expel them from the community.

Indeed, most modern scholars suspect that deep-seated guilt about practicing white magic and the fear of getting caught weighed heavily on the young women, especially on Abigail and the older girls. Certainly they, like other Puritan children, had been systematically and thoroughly programmed with a strong fear of evil, the devil, demons, witches, and so forth. Puritan children commonly and frequently heard lectures and sermons warning of the dire consequences for young people who broke the rules of family and society. Typical were the following words aimed at young people by Cotton Mather in one of his children's books:

They which lie [and commit other such offenses] must go to their father, the devil, into everlasting burning; they which never pray,

OBSERVATIONS

As well *Historical* as *Theological*, upon the NATURE, the NUMBER, and the OPERATIONS of the

DEVILS.

Accompany'd with,

I. Some Accounts of the Grievous Molestations, by DÆMONS and WITCHCRAFTS, which have lately annoy'd the Countrey; and the Trials of some eminent *Malefactors* Executed upon occasion thereof: with several Remarkable *Curiosities* therein occurring.

II. Some Counsils, Directing a due Improvement of the terrible things, lately done, by the Unusual & Amazing Range of EVIL SPIRITS, in Our Neighbourhood: & the methods to prevent the *Wrongs* which those *Evil Angels* may intend against all sorts of people among us; especially in Accusations of the Innocent.

III. Some Conjectures upon the great EVENTS, likely to befall, the WORLD in General, and NEW-ENGLAND in Particular; as also upon the Advances of the TIME, when we shall see BETTER DAYES.

IV A short Narrative of a late Outrage committed by a knot of WITCHES in *Swedeland*, very much Resembling, and so far Explaining, *That* under which our parts of *America* have laboured!

V THE DEVIL DISCOVERED: In a Brief Discourse upon those TEMPTATIONS, which are the more Ordinary *Devices* of the Wicked One.

By **Cotton Mather**.

Boston Printed by *Benj. Harris* for *Sam. Phillips.* 1693.

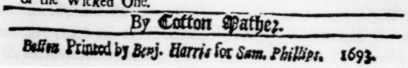

A chapter on devils from Cotton Mather's book, The Wonders of the Invisible World. *In seventeenth-century Puritan society, magic was thought to be the devil's work.*

Historians speculate that it could have been the fear of going to hell that drove Abigail Williams and Betty Parris to display their unusual behaviors.

God will pour out his wrath upon them; and when they bed and pray in hell fire, God will not forgive them, but there [they] must lie forever. Are you willing to go to hell and burn with the devil and his [evil] angels?[15]

Abigail Williams and her playmates likely had already heard diatribes like this hundreds of times in their young lives. And nagging fear of eternal damnation was almost certainly an ever-present part of their worldview. Modern physicians and psychologists have shown that such deep-seated fears can, in some people, manifest themselves in debilitating physical symptoms.

Whatever their personal motivations may have been, early in February 1692 the girls in Tituba's circle began displaying such symptoms. It appears that Betty and Abigail were the first to be afflicted. Reverend and Mrs. Parris noticed that the girls were cowering in corners, entering trancelike states, and uttering meaningless words and phrases. Worst of all, like Anne Cole in Hartford and the Goodwin children in Boston, Betty and Abigail started throwing fits. Deodat Lawson, a Puritan minister who visited Salem that winter, described the following incident at the Parris house:

In the beginning of the evening I went to pay Mr. Parris a visit. When I was there, his kinswoman, Abigail Williams . . . had a grievous fit. She was at first harried with violence to and fro in the room . . . sometimes making as if she would fly, stretching up her arms as high as she could, and crying, "Whish, Whish, Whish!" several times. [She then claimed she saw an invisible witch in the room.] After that, she ran to the fire and began to throw firebrands about the house and [to] run . . . as if she would run up [the] chimney.[16]

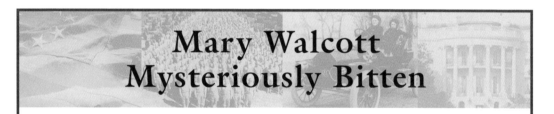

Mary Walcott Mysteriously Bitten

Deodat Lawson, who served as parson in Salem Village before Reverend Samuel Parris assumed that post, later described a disturbing incident involving one of the afflicted girls, Mary Walcott:

On the nineteenth day of March last, I went to Salem Village, and lodged at Nathaniel Ingersoll's near to minister Parris's house, and presently, after I came into my lodging, Captain Walcott's daughter, Mary, came to Lieutenant Ingersoll's and spoke to me. But suddenly afterward, as she stood by the door, [she] was bitten so that she cried of her wrist [being bitten], and looking on it with a candle, we saw apparently the marks of teeth, both upper and lower set, on each side of her wrist.

Quoted in Piney.com, "Deodat Lawson's *A Brief and True Narrative*." www.piney.com/ColDeoLawSurp.html.

Soon the rest of the girls in Tituba's circle were displaying the same sorts of symptoms, including violent fits. Meanwhile, one of their number, Mary Walcott, appeared to have been bitten by some invisible entity, and Elizabeth Hubbard claimed she had been stalked by a pack of wolves, creatures widely associated with evil.

The Witch Cake

The parents of the afflicted girls were, quite understandably, disturbed and concerned by these odd behaviors and incidents. Parris at first ordered Betty and Abigail to fast and pray. He hoped that these traditional religious rituals would make the strange symptoms go away. When this approach did not work, Parris took the girls to Dr. Griggs and other Puritan physicians. After a thorough examination, Griggs pronounced that Betty and Abigail must be "under an evil hand."[17] In other words, the devil, a witch, or some other evil being was causing their weird symptoms. This is not surprising. First, he and other doctors of his day knew almost nothing about psychological traumas and ailments. Also, he had the case of the Goodwin children as a precedent; their fits had been "proven" to be caused by evil beings, he reasoned, so the Parris girls' fits must have the same cause.

Meanwhile, the girls' fits became more frequent and dramatic. Interestingly, this happened only after people from outlying farms, as well as Salem Town, started congregating in the village, eager to witness the young women's afflictions.

It was as if the girls enjoyed being the center of attention and gave the crowds more of what they came to see. They even began having convulsions in church on Sunday. Again, in retrospect it is revealing that the episodes in church occurred only during lulls in the services; perhaps the girls feared severe retribution by God if they interrupted the formal prayers and sermons.

Extremely concerned, Mary Walcott's aunt, Mary Sibley, decided to try eradicating the girls' evil spells using a traditional English remedy. It involved baking a witch cake, consisting of flour mixed with the urine of the suspected victim of a witch. According to some European folk beliefs, an evil spell might be broken if one fed the cake to an animal thought to be a familiar, a witch's helper. At the same time, the identity of the offending witch would be revealed.

Guided by Sibley, John Indian (or perhaps his wife Tituba) baked the witch cake, and they fed it to the Parris family's dog. (Dogs were commonly thought to be witches' familiars.) Reverend Parris later reprimanded Goodwife Sibley, saying that she had rashly used the devil's tools to combat the devil. He even forced her to apologize to the entire community in church.

The witch cake had failed to stop the fits and other disturbing behaviors of Salem Village's afflicted girls. However, the girls knew about the cake and were aware that it was designed in part to identify the witch or witches that were tormenting them. Perhaps that is why on February 26, the day after the cake incident, Betty and Abigail

The Power of Suggestion

A number of modern observers think that the power of suggestion likely played an integral part in the initial naming of witches by the afflicted girls of Salem Village. At first, the girls claimed they did not know who was harassing them. Only after their elders asked about specific people, persons already disliked in the community, did the girls agree that those named were witches. As Marion L. Starkey, a noted scholar of the Salem trials, writes:

The simple "Who torments you?" had been proved ineffectual. Leading questions were now put to the girls. . . . Names of old suspects were now suggested to the girls and their reactions sharply studied. Parris for his part found his mind turning to Tituba. Now that he looked back, he recalled that Betty and Abigail had been with the untutored slave more often than was good for them. . . . So the questions were put, and locked though the girls were in their own private world, in the hypnoid state to which they periodically achieved they could not indefinitely remain impervious to the power of such persistent suggestion.

Marion L. Starkey, *The Devil in Massachusetts: A Modern Enquiry into the Salem Witch Trials.* New York: Random House, 1989, pp. 47–48.

first accused a specific person of being a witch. They claimed Tituba was the evil witch causing their pain. The very next day, Ann Putnam and other afflicted girls began naming names, too. They accused two older women in the village—Sarah Good and Sarah Osborne—of being witches. In this way, the hysterical behavior of a few misguided young women began to infect their community with unreasoning fear and to ruin the reputations and lives of hundreds of innocent people.

Chapter Three

The First Accused Witches Are Questioned

On February 26 and 27, 1692, some of the Salem Village girls who had been displaying odd physical symptoms accused three local women of practicing witchcraft. The accused were the Caribbean slave Tituba and two aging matrons, Sarah Good and Sarah Osborne. News of the accusations spread rapidly through the village. And several concerned citizens wasted little time in taking action. Nothing of a legal nature could be done on February 28 because it was a Sunday, and both Salem Village and Salem Town came to a virtual standstill on the Sabbath. But early the next day, February 29, four men of the village met and began the arduous trek to Salem Town to lodge formal complaints against the three women. One of these men was Ann Putnam's father, Thomas; the others were Thomas's brother Edward and farmers Joseph Hutchinson and Thomas Preston.

Reaching the town before noon, the men denounced Tituba, Sarah Good, and Sarah Osborne to two magistrates. Later that day, these officials, John Hathorne and Jonathan Corwin, issued arrest warrants for the three women.

Armed with these warrants, the next day two constables rounded up Tituba, Sarah Good, and Sarah Osborne and brought them to Nathaniel Ingersoll's tavern in the center of Salem Village. (The tavern sometimes doubled as an official meetinghouse.) There, the three women were to be questioned by Hathorne and Corwin to determine if there was enough evidence to hold them for trial.

These events marked the beginning of the ominous preliminary period of the Salem witch hysteria. During the ensuing three months, a growing number of women and men would be accused of witchcraft, questioned, and jailed pending the appointing of judges and setup of a court in the colony. Sadly, the trials would, legally speaking, turn out to be mere formalities. Given the highly restrictive, fearful, and paranoid social and political climate of Puritan society, those accused during the pretrial period were automatically assumed to be guilty. The ultimate question would not be whether or not they were witches, but how severe their punishments would be.

Inevitable Suspects

In retrospect, it is clear that the initial accusations of witchcraft were heavily guided by the fear, ignorance, cruelty, and lack of charity inherent in Puritan society. History has shown that such societies tend to hold suspect, shun, isolate, and persecute the weakest and/or least conformist of their own members. Certainly it is no coincidence that the first people accused of being witches were not well-to-do citizens with sterling reputations and connections in high places. Nor is it surprising that at first no men were accused; after all, men were seen as the community's leading citizens and the guardians and enforcers of order and conformity.

Many people who accused others of witchcraft displayed odd physical symptoms, such as fainting for no reason.

The front exterior of the courthouse where the Salem witch trials were held.

Rather, the initial targets were older women whose reputations were already questionable. As women, they were assumed from the start to be weak, gullible, corruptible, and more susceptible than men to falling under the control of evil forces. Another black mark against these women was that they were physically unattractive and aging; Puritan society looked askance at women whose faces were wrinkled, whose flesh was sagging, and whose bodies were stooped by years of backbreaking work. Still another reason to suspect the women was their outspokenness. People, particularly women, who complained too much, asked too many questions, or said or did things that the community deemed even slightly out of the ordinary were seen as troublemakers and potential agents of sin and evil. Such women, Carol F. Karlsen points out, "risked not only society's vengeance, but also the loss of approval and love of the people closest to them—most particularly their own fathers."[18] The fact that the women were poor and economically and politically powerless also made them easy targets.

Tituba, the first to be accused of practicing witchcraft, conveniently fit all of these criteria. Not only was she a woman, she was foreign-born, had dark skin, and spoke with a discernible accent. Moreover, Tituba hailed from a non-Christian society that had, by English and Puritan standards, strange, unwholesome customs, including some associated with magic and evil beings. Considering these attributes, in any witch hunt in a white Christian community, the woman from Barbados "was an inevitable suspect," as Marion L. Starkey puts it.

> If Salem Village contained anyone at all who deliberately practiced the black arts, it was she. That the girls did not indict her earlier . . . can only have been due to a not unreasonable fear of what Tituba, under cross-examination, might say about them. Guilt is an indispensable ingredient in the witch's broth of hysteria.[19]

The second victim of the witch hysteria, Sarah Good, also bore, in addition to her gender, a number of social black marks that made her a likely suspect. First, she was poor and lived in disgrace

Sarah Good, accused of being a witch, was hanged in 1692.

on the fringes of the community. Her poverty had been the result of a series of financial disasters during her two marriages, which had left her a destitute beggar. Her disgrace derived in part from the suicide of her father, John Solart, in 1672, an act roundly condemned by Puritans of all walks of life. Sarah Good's physical appearance also made her a natural suspect in the witch hunt. Though she was only around forty, her hard life had taken a toll, and she looked closer to seventy, with a bent back, wrinkled face, prematurely gray hair, and a raspy voice. In other words, she looked and sounded like the stereotype of a witch.

Sarah Osborne, the third woman the girls accused of being a witch, had also had a difficult life. Her prosperous first husband, Robert Prince, had died, after which she had married her penniless indentured servant, John Osborne. Later, she had become disabled; and by the time she was accused of witchcraft, she was sixty-nine, poverty-stricken, badly wrinkled, and bedridden. Because of her physical infirmity, Sarah Osborne could not make it to church on Sundays. This was another black mark against her, as Puritan elders expected everyone to attend services, no matter how physically incapacitated they might be.

The First Round of Questioning

On the morning of Tuesday, March 1, 1692, as Sarah Osborne, Sarah Good, and Tituba were led to Ingersoll's tavern, the weather in the region of Salem was finally clearing after nearly a week of storms. Though many of the roads in the area were flooded and impassable, hundreds of people flocked from all around to witness the questioning. In fact, the crowd became so large that the tavern could not hold them all; so the magistrates in charge of the proceedings, Hathorne and Corwin, decided to move them to the nearby meetinghouse.

Although the questioning was a serious legal procedure, neither of these officials had any formal legal training. This was partly because at the time the only professional school in the colony—Harvard College—prepared young men for the ministry only. Also, there simply were no qualified lawyers in Massachusetts Bay. "The Puritans had a low opinion of lawyers," Starkey points out,

> and did not permit the professional practice of law in the colony. In effect, the administration of the law was in the hands of laymen, most of them second-generation colonists who had an incomplete grasp of current principles of English jurisdiction.[20]

Under these circumstances, the accused women were at still another disadvantage, namely they lacked legal rights and representation. The men in charge of both the questioning sessions and trials had little understanding of the venerable old English idea that an accused person is innocent until proven guilty. Moreover, none of the public officials who ran these proceedings "saw any reason to provide an accused witch with right of counsel," Starkey adds.

The Puritans Establish Harvard

Although colonial Puritan society was extremely narrow-minded and strict, both religiously and socially, the Puritans placed a strong emphasis on education. They held that both men and women needed to be educated to a certain degree so that they could properly study the Bible. To that end, in 1635 members of the Massachusetts Bay Colony established the first public school in America—Boston Latin School. They also set up America's first college—Harvard College—in 1636. At first, the purpose of Harvard was to train local colonial ministers so that fewer churchmen would have to be imported from England. In time, however, the college offered courses in all the liberal arts, including mathematics and philosophy. It is perhaps ironic that the same society that demonstrated its ignorance by persecuting people for witchcraft created a school that became one of the most progressive, enlightened educational institutions in the world.

In 1636 members of the Massachusetts Bay Colony established Harvard College.

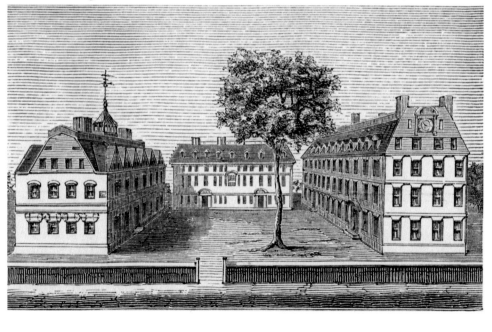

The questioning of many accused witches took place at the Salem meetinghouse.

"And their notions of evidence and of courtroom etiquette were, to put it mildly, peculiar."[21]

Thus, when Hathorne began the first round of questioning, singling out Sarah Good, he did not conduct himself as an impartial fact gatherer, as would have been the fair and proper approach. Instead, he acted like a zealous prosecutor who is certain the suspect is guilty and is eager to force a confession from her. "Sarah Good," he began with a stern voice and intimidating tone, "what evil spirit have you familiarity with?"

"None," the woman answered, doing her best to keep her composure in front of the gawking, largely hostile crowd.

"Have you made no contact with the devil?" Hathorne asked.

"No."

"Why do you hurt these children?" He indicated Betty Parris, Abigail Williams, Ann Putnam, and Elizabeth Hubbard, all of whom were sitting nearby.

"I do not hurt them," Good answered. "I scorn it."

"Who do you employ, then, to do it?"

"I employ nobody," she retorted, bravely holding her ground.

"What creature do you employ, then?"

"No creature. But I am falsely accused."[22]

In the moments that followed, the magistrate asked Betty and the other girls if they were sure that this woman, Sarah Good, was their tormentor. The girls insisted that she was. Furthermore, they said, Good had harassed them that very morning by sending her specter, or invisible evil spirit, to pinch and assault them.

"'Do you see now what you have done?' Hathorne asked Good. 'Why do you not tell us the truth? Why do you thus torment these poor children?'

"'I do not torment them,' the woman insisted."[23] And so it went. Good remained steadfast that she was innocent. But the magistrates, in their narrow-minded rush to judgment, decided that she must be lying and therefore should be held for trial.

A Victim Rather than a Perpetrator?

Sarah Osborne was next to be questioned. Hathorne asked her some of the same initial questions he had asked Sarah Good, beginning with: "What evil spirit have you familiarity with?" Osborne declared that she had no such familiarity, nor had she ever seen the devil, nor consorted with any of the devil's helpers. Then Hathorne abruptly changed the direction of the questioning. "What familiarity do you have with Sarah Good," he demanded. Clearly, he was seeking to incriminate the present suspect by linking her with the other accused woman. "None," Osborne replied. "I have not seen her in these two years." She went on to explain that the last encounter she had had with Sarah Good was

A group of Puritans arrests an accused witch from Salem, Massachusetts.

one day when the two had seen each other on the road to Salem Town. They had merely exchanged brief hellos, Osborne claimed, and continued on their separate ways. "Sarah Good said that it was you who hurt the children," Hathorne suddenly told Osborne. She retorted: "I do not know that the devil goes about in my likeness to do any hurt."[24]

Next, as he had done earlier while questioning Sarah Good, Hathorne addressed himself to the afflicted girls. He asked them to confirm that Sarah Osborne had tormented them, and they replied in the affirmative. At this point, Osborne asserted that she was not only innocent, but also more likely to be the victim rather than the perpetrator of witchcraft. When Hathorne asked what she meant, she told him how she once had dreamed that she saw an ominous form resembling a black-skinned Indian near her bed. It had pinched her and pulled her hair. Perhaps this was an evil creature sent by the devil to harass her.

Finally, the questioner attempted to blacken Osborne's image and reputation by emphasizing her lack of church attendance. She insisted that poor health had kept her from attending services. But this did not satisfy Hathorne and Corwin. They decided that she, like Sarah Good, should be held for trial.

Tituba's Pivotal Testimony

The last woman to be questioned that day was the slave Tituba. She had already been a subject of unusually great interest in the community because of her dark skin and foreign origins. But after Sarah Osborne's testimony about having been tormented by a black-skinned Indian, the crowd was even more interested to hear what Tituba, who fit that description, had to say.

At first, the slave woman claimed that she had done the children no harm. But then her testimony took a decidedly different turn, as she increasingly admitted her involvement in supernatural affairs. Exactly why she confessed to aiding in witchcraft is uncertain, but some experts suggest that she had been coached by Samuel Parris and Thomas Putnam, who wanted her to implicate Good and Osborne. "Four women sometimes hurt the children," Tituba told Hathorne and Corwin. When asked to name them, she answered Sarah Good, Sarah Osborne, and two other women who came to Salem from Boston accompanied by a strange tall man. In a long round of questioning, Tituba claimed that the four witches had been aided by several evil animals, including a black dog, a yellow bird, and some cats. All the witches and animals had sometimes taken spectral, or invisible, forms. Then Hathorne concentrated on the tall man. "What clothes does the man appear to you in?" he inquired. "Black clothes sometimes,"[25] Tituba said. The implication, one that everyone in the room must have gathered, was that this tall man in black clothes was the devil himself.

Suddenly, Betty and Abigail began having convulsions, causing murmurs of astonishment and fear to ripple through the room. Hathorne quickly used this

Tituba's Evil Animals

During magistrate John Hathorne's questioning of Tituba on March 1, 1692, she described how the devil and/or his followers took the forms of a number of animals:

Hathorne: Other likenesses besides a man have appeared to you?

Tituba: Sometimes like a hog. Sometimes like a great black dog.

Hathorne: What did they say unto you?

Tituba: They told me [to] serve him [the devil] and that was a good way; I told him I was afraid [of the black dog], [and] he told me he would be worse then to me.

Hathorne: What did you say to him after that?

Tituba: I answered: I will Serve you no longer. He told me he would do me hurt then.

Hathorne: What other creatures have you seen? . . .

Tituba: A little yellow bird. . . . [Also] I saw 2 cats, one red, another black [and] as big as a little dog.

Hathorne: What did these cats do? . . .

Tituba: They did scratch me.

Quoted in *Salem Witchcraft Trials, 1692,* Famous American Trials, "Examination of Tituba." www.law. umkc.edu/faculty/projects/ftrials/salem/ASA_TITX.HTM.

outburst to his advantage, asking Tituba, "Do you see who it is who torments these children now?" "Yes," she readily replied. "It is Goody Good. She hurts them in her own shape."[26] Then Tituba herself seemed to become speechless and threw a fit similar to that performed by the girls. Eventually composing herself, the slave woman blurted out that she had just been assaulted by the specters of Good and Osborne.

Tituba's testimony, whoever had coached it, proved pivotal because it did irreparable harm to Sarah Good and Sarah Osborne, as well as to the community. First, the slave woman had confirmed community-wide suspicions and distrust of Good and Osborne. Also, Tituba had said that other witches were loose in the region, a revelation that significantly increased the witch hysteria that already existed in Salem. From that moment on, nearly everyone was on the lookout for evil witches in their midst.

As for the three women, for the time being they were sent to a jail in Boston. The already ill and frail Sarah Osborne died there two months later, but Sarah Good was destined to stand trial for witchcraft. Meanwhile, because Tituba had confessed and told the magistrates what they wanted to hear, they did not bind her over for trial, but merely imprisoned her.

New Suspects Needed

Early evidence that the wave of hysteria in Salem Village was growing came only a few days after Sarah Good, Sarah Osborne, and Tituba were carted off to prison. The afflicted girls continued to have seizure-like fits. But what was causing them now? In theory, if witchcraft was real, the specters of the imprisoned women could easily have floated from Boston to Salem and continued to harass the girls. But evidently this did not occur to Betty, Abigail, Ann, and the other children; in their minds, their accused tormentors were gone, so new suspects were needed to explain their continued fits and other symptoms.

Accordingly, on March 11, 1692, Ann Putnam claimed that she was being tormented by Martha Corey, an upstanding member of the community and a regular churchgoer. Thomas Putnam and some other men went to Corey's house on March 12 and questioned her informally. Then, on March 21, she was forced to appear for formal questioning at Ingersoll's tavern. According to the later report of the Reverend Deodat Lawson, three

The exterior of the old witch jail and dungeon in Salem, Massachusetts.

Arrest Warrant for a Suspected Witch

The magistrates in Salem Town issued numerous arrest warrants during the roundup of suspected witches from late February through May 1692. Most of these warrants looked identical or similar to this one for the arrest of Martha Corey, dated March 19, 1692:

There being complaint this day made before us, by Edward Putnam and Henry Kenney, yeomen both of Salem Village, against Martha Corey, the wife of Giles Corey of Salem Farms, for suspicion of having committed sundry [diverse] acts of witchcraft and thereby done much hurt and injury unto the body of Ann Putnam . . . the daughter of said Thomas Putnam, and . . . also Abigail Williams, one of Mr. Parris's family. . . . You are therefore in their Majesties' names hereby required to apprehend and bring before us Martha Corey . . . on Monday next, being the 21st day of this instant [present] month, at the house of Lt. Nathaniel Ingersoll of Salem Village, [at] about twelve of the clock in the day [i.e., noon] in order to [conduct] her examination.

Quoted in Electronic Text Center, University of Virginia Library, *The Salem Witchcraft Papers*, vol. 1, "Warrant for Arrest of Martha Corey." http://etext.virginia.edu/etcbin/toccer-new2?id=BoySal1.sgm&images =images/modeng&data=/texts/english/modeng/oldsalem&tag=public&part=208&division=div2.

---

of the supposedly bewitched girls "vehemently accused [Corey] in the assembly of afflicting them, by biting, pinching, strangling, etc. And they did in their fit see her likeness [i.e., her specter] coming to them."[27] In spite of Corey's repeated protestations of innocence, the magistrates were satisfied that she must be a witch and ordered her thrown into jail to await trial.

The accusations of witchcraft did not end with Martha Corey. On March 19, Abigail Williams claimed that the specter of another respectable churchgoer, Rebecca Nurse, was tormenting her. Some of the other afflicted girls soon confirmed that Nurse was a witch. So on March 24, the seventy-one-year-old woman was arrested and brought to the village meetinghouse for questioning. The proceedings turned into a raucous spectacle as the girls staged numerous fits, each time claiming that Rebecca Nurse's specter was assaulting them. Not surprisingly, she, too, was sent off to jail. That same day, Dorcas Good, the four-year-old daughter of Sarah Good, went on display in the meetinghouse after being denounced as a witch; the defenseless child, who had no real idea of what was happening, soon ended up in prison with the other accused witches.

Some residents of Salem now felt that the witch hunt had gone too far. They showed the courage to doubt the claims made by the afflicted girls and immediately paid a heavy price for it. One of these brave individuals was farmer John Procter, whose servant, Mary Warren, was among the girls having fits. When he said that all the girls deserved a good thrashing and indicated that he might whip the truth out of Mary, the girls promptly accused his wife, Elizabeth, of being a witch. John Procter strenuously objected and as a result was himself accused of witchcraft and arrested.

Similarly, when Rebecca Nurse's sister, Sarah Cloyse, stormed out of church one day to protest the recent arrests, she,

Accused witch Martha Corey in her jail cell.

Rebecca Nurse's Testimony

Part of Hathorne's questioning of Rebecca Nurse, which occurred on March 24, went this way:

Hathorne: Tell us, have you not had invisible appearances more than what is common in nature?

Nurse: I have none, nor never had [any] in my life.

Hathorne: Do you think these [afflicted girls] suffer voluntarily or involuntarily?

Nurse: I cannot tell.

Hathorne: That is strange. Everyone can judge.

Nurse: I must be silent.

Hathorne: They accuse you of hurting them, and if you think it is not unwillingly, but by design [i.e., that they are faking their fits], you must look upon them as murderers [since convicted witches were usually executed].

Nurse: I cannot tell what to think of it. . . .

Hathorne: Do you think these [girls] suffer against their wills or not?

Nurse: I do not think [they] suffer against their wills.

Quoted in Marilynne K. Roach, *The Salem Witch Trials: A Day-by-Day Chronicle of a Community Under Siege.* New York: Taylor Trade, 2002, p. 54.

too, was accused and arrested. The circle of accusations and arrests was widening at an alarming rate and there seemed no end in sight. A remark John Procter had made shortly before his arrest now seemed to ring true with a vengeance. If the afflicted girls were allowed to continue making their fantastic accusations, he had said, "we should all be [labeled] devils and witches quickly."[28]

Chapter Four

The Infamous Witch Trials Begin

The formal legal proceedings known as the Salem witch trials began in Salem Town early in June 1692. By that time, all of eastern Massachusetts was in an uproar, as during April and May the witch hysteria that had begun in late February had nearly reached its height. Like a creeping, deadly plague, fear, accusations, and arrest warrants spread outward to other towns in the colony. People were arrested in Malden, Lynn, Beverly, Marblehead, Charleston, Boston, and Andover, among others. No one seemed safe, as neighbors accused neighbors and friends denounced friends. As a result, by the last day of May nearly a hundred people swelled the colony's jails, most of them suspected of being witches and awaiting trial.

Part of this colony-wide fixation with witches can be attributed to the ignorance and fear of the populace. After all, just about everyone believed in the real-ity of witches and witchcraft and feared that the devil was actively trying to corrupt people. However, the hysteria undoubtedly also stemmed in part from the fact that an increasing number of people had personal stakes in proving that the accused witches were both real and guilty. Consider the example of the afflicted girls. They surely realized that they faced severe punishment if their damning accusations proved to be wrong or if they were exposed as fakers. In a different vein, Thomas Putnam and several other local landowners stood to profit handsomely from lands and goods confiscated from jailed and executed witches. As for Hathorne and the other magistrates, they had laid their credibility on the line during the preliminary questioning sessions; their reputations would surely be damaged or ruined if those they had firmly denounced as witches were somehow to be found innocent during the upcoming trials.

One telling example of how the witch hysteria was to some degree manipulated by these major participants was the case of one of the afflicted girls, twenty-year-old Mary Warren. When John Procter threatened to beat the truth out of her, Warren suddenly stopped having fits and said that she no longer saw any specters of witches. Hearing this, the other girls instantly turned on her and accused her of joining forces with the devil.

After questioning, Warren spent three weeks in jail, where the magistrates repeatedly visited her. They steadily coerced her and wore her down until she

Illustration of a witchcraft trial in Salem Village in the 1690s.

admitted that she had been corrupted by the devil and did see specters of witches, especially those of John and Elizabeth Procter. Then the magistrates quietly released the confused, conflicted young woman and allowed her to rejoin Abigail Williams and the other girls, who were in the midst of accusing still more people of practicing witchcraft. Clearly, Mary Warren had learned that as long as she acted as the magistrates and afflicted girls wanted and expected her to, she would remain safe and unharmed.

Thus, the Salem witch trials began under a toxic cloud of fear, paranoia, greed, hypocrisy, and naked self-preservation. These feelings and motivations had to be vented, by both selected individuals and society as a whole. And the only realistic way that could happen was to give all the vested parties what they wanted—some formal convictions and executions. In short, the witch hysteria that gripped Salem and Massachusetts Bay was not likely to dissipate until the blood of the innocent had been spilled. And indeed, the trials and brutal executions of Sarah Good, Rebecca Nurse, and others who were clearly not witches would soon confirm this grim reality.

Appointing a Court and Judges

As for the trials themselves, by law they could not begin until the Massachusetts Bay Colony had a new charter from England. The colony's original charter had lapsed three years before, leaving its inhabitants in a sort of legal limbo in which no legally sanctioned trials could

be conducted. To remedy this situation, the widely respected minister Increase Mather had recently journeyed to England to petition the government for a new colonial charter. He returned in mid-May 1692 with the charter in hand, which meant that the trials could begin shortly afterward.

Mather brought with him a new colonial governor, William Phipps, whose authority was needed to set up the court and appoint its judges. Phipps arrived to see the local jails overflowing and realized that he had his work cut out for him. In a letter addressed to his superiors in England, he wrote:

> When I first arrived, I found this province miserably harassed with a most horrible witchcraft or possession of devils, which had broke in upon several towns. Some scores of poor people were taken with preternatural torments. . . . There were many committed to the prison upon suspicion of witchcraft before my arrival. The loud cries and clamors of the friends of the afflicted people . . . and many others prevailed with me to give a commission of Oyer and Terminer for discovering what witchcraft might be at the bottom [of this turmoil].[29]

The "Oyer and Terminer" Phipps mentioned was an old Anglo-French legal phrase that meant "to hear and determine." It referred to a special court convened to hear criminal cases. Phipps authorized the creation of the court in

The title page to Tales of Conscience Concerning Evil Spirits *by Increase Mather.*

early June and selected seven judges. One was the deputy (or lieutenant) governor, William Stoughton, who resided in Dorchester. The others were Bostonians John Richards, William Sergeant, Samuel Sewall, and Wait Winthrop, along with Nathaniel Saltonstall from Haverhill and Bartholomew Gedney from Salem.

In a later letter home, Phipps stated: "I depended on the court for a right method of proceeding in cases of witchcraft."[30] By "method," Phipps meant the kinds of evidence that would be admissible in the witchcraft trials. At the time, based on precedent in earlier such cases in the colony and in England, several kinds of evidence were allowed that today would be viewed as highly prejudiced, even nonsensical. For example, one kind of evidence that supposedly proved someone was an agent of the devil was his or her inability to recite the Lord's Prayer without error. Also, if someone who had confessed to being a witch (as Tituba had) proceeded to

The New Governor on Supernatural Forces

In a letter sent in October 1692 to his superiors in England, William Phipps, the new governor of the Massachusetts Bay Colony, tried his best to describe the strange situation in which a number of local girls had seizures that seemed to be caused by supernatural forces. Phipps said in part:

The court still proceeded in the same method of trying [the witches], which was by the evidence of the afflicted persons, who when they were brought into the court . . . instantly fell to the ground in strange agonies and grievous torments, but when touched by them upon the arm or some other part of their flesh they immediately revived and came to themselves. . . . When I enquired into the matter, I was informed by the judges that they begin with this [evidence of the fits], but [also] had human testimony against such [persons] as were condemned and undoubted proof of their being witches, but at length I found that the devil did take upon him the shape of innocent persons.

Quoted in Frances Hill, ed., *The Salem Witch Trials Reader*. New York: Da Capo, 2000, p. 102.

accuse someone else of the same, it was seen as acceptable evidence. There was also spectral evidence—that is, claims made by various persons that they had witnessed invisible specters harassing people. (Oddly, few seemed to question the fact that some people could see these apparitions, while others could not.)

Other kinds of acceptable evidence in witchcraft cases involved the discovery of physical proof on the bodies of the accused. As a matter of course, a defendant was taken into a room, stripped naked, and closely examined. If a small red circle was found on his or her skin, it was deemed to be the "mark of the devil." A "pin test" was then performed, in which the examiner pierced the red mark with a pin. If it did not bleed, it was viewed as another sign of the devil's work. In the case of another kind of evidence, the "touch test," the accused was forced to touch someone who was having a witchcraft-induced fit. If the fit suddenly stopped, it supposedly proved that the specter afflicting the victim had jumped back into the body of the accused; therefore the accused was guilty.

The Court Hears Its First Witchcraft Case

As it turned out, a very different use of pins became evidence of witchcraft in the initial case tried by the court of Oyer and Terminer when it convened on June 2.

William Stoughton was selected to be a judge for the witchcraft trials.

William Stacey's Testimony

Among the witnesses who testified against Bridget Bishop was William Stacey, whose father ran a colonial mill. Stacey testified in part:

About fourteen years ago, [I] was visited with the Small Pox, then Bridget Bishop did give [me] a visit, and . . . professed a great love for [me] in [my] affliction. . . . Some time after [I] was well, the said Bishop got [me] to do some work for her, for which she gave [me] three pense. . . . But [I] had not gone [far] before [I] looked in [my] pocket [and] could not find any [of the money]. . . . Some time after this, [I was] in a dark night going to the barn [when I] was suddenly taken or hoisted from the ground [by some invisible agent] and thrown against a stone wall, [then] after that taken up again and thrown down a bank [embankment].

Quoted in Electronic Text Center, University of Virginia Library, *The Salem Witchcraft Papers*, vol. 1, "William Stacy v. Bridget Bishop." http://etext.virginia.edu/etcbin/toccer-new2?id=BoySal1.sgm&images=images/modeng&data=/texts/english/modeng/oldsalem&tag=public&part=36&division=div2.

The first person to be tried as a witch in Salem was Bridget Bishop, a tavern keeper in her late sixties or early seventies. From the paranoid point of view of Puritan society, Bishop had a number of black marks against her that had made her an inevitable suspect in the witch hysteria. About twelve years before, she had been accused of evil doings, though she had never been legally tried. Rumors had it that she had bewitched some horses and turned herself into a cat.

There was also damning testimony from a number of Bishop's neighbors and acquaintances, who recounted strange events that happened when she was around. One modern expert on the trials summarizes the testimony of William Stacey, the son of a Salem mill operator:

Coins disappeared from his pocket after she paid him for work. His cart became stuck in a hole right after he told her how some folk suspected she was a witch, only there was no hole. He then talked . . . about the time her specter invaded his room. . . . Stacey testified about her stealing his father's brass [a metal object from the family mill], after which he got tossed against a stone wall and down a bank one night. After that, his cart collapsed entirely the next time he passed her. But worse yet, his daughter Priscilla, a healthy child, fell ill and died within two weeks.[31]

Stacey's testimony was typical of the witch hysteria and trials of the period. It was quite common to blame ordinary accidents and unfortunate events, including naturally occurring deaths, on suspected witches.

Though the testimony given against Bishop by Stacey and other neighbors was damaging, the court was most swayed by the so-called evidence found by workmen who had helped to renovate a house Bishop had lived in a few years before. They claimed they had torn "down the cellar wall of the old house," and "in holes in the old wall" they had "found several puppets made up of rags and hogs' bristles with headless pins in them with the points outward."[32] Now commonly called voodoo dolls, miniature images pierced with pins had long been standard instruments of black magic in Europe and elsewhere. Supposedly, a puppet represented one's enemy,

and when one pricked the puppet with a pin, that enemy suffered harm.

When asked about the puppets hidden in the wall, Bridget Bishop claimed she had no idea how they got there. But the judges and twelve men making up the jury did not believe her, partly because they already assumed she must be guilty. As in all the cases heard in the Salem witch trials, the initial questionings determined the suspects' guilt. The court trials constituted little more than legal rubber stamps confirming that guilt. Thus, no one was surprised when the court found Bishop guilty of being a witch and sentenced her to be executed.

On Gallows Hill

Another aspect of the Salem trials that differs from modern legal proceedings is that those found guilty had no recourse

Witches' Hill in Salem Village, Massachusetts, was where many accused witches were put to death.

to legal appeals and received no mercy of any kind. Today in the United States, because of an extended series of appeals, an execution takes place several years after the convicted person is sentenced. In seventeenth-century Salem, in stark contrast, justice, if it can be called that, was much swifter. On June 10, 1692, only eight days after her trial, Bridget Bishop was taken to Gallows Hill (later called Witches' Hill), located not far southwest of Salem Town.

The other eighteen victims who later received the same sentence were doomed to undergo essentially the same procedure that Bishop did on that gloomy Massachusetts morning. First, her hands were bound tightly and she was placed in a wooden cart. A constable drove the cart down the town's main street while guards rode alongside to keep the onlookers at bay. There were hundreds of these spectators, who had come from all the neighboring towns to take a ghoulish sort of delight in seeing someone suffer in their death pangs. Most members of the crowd cruelly shouted at and mocked the prisoner as the cart made its way to the hill of death. One local man, Nathaniel Cary, who pitied the condemned individuals, later wrote a letter to the magistrates complaining about the vicious and heartless conduct of the spectators. "To speak of their usage of the prisoners," he said, "and the inhumanity shown to them of the time of their execution, no sober Christian could bear. They had also [in addition to their court trials] trials of cruel mockings."[33]

When the cart, still surrounded by jeering people, reached Gallows Hill, Bridget Bishop was removed and escorted up the side of the hill. At the summit, a ladder had been set up beneath a stout branch of a large oak tree, from which a noosed rope hung. An executioner stood by. He placed a cloth hood over the condemned woman's head and dragged her up the ladder, where he placed the noose around her neck. Then, while she proclaimed her innocence one last time, he pushed her off the ladder so that her body swung sideways and downward. In most of these executions, the bodies did not drop with enough force to break the victims' necks; therefore, they slowly strangled to death. In Marilynne K. Roach's words:

In these cases, the face beneath the hood suffused dark red from the dammed up blood that wept from eyes, nose, and mouth. Starved lungs rasped loudly for the air they could no longer breathe. The whole body thrashed against its bonds as it convulsed uncontrollably, clenching and unclenching in every part. . . . After a last jerk, the body stilled, empty of life at last.[34]

In this pitiless way, Bridget Bishop died. The extreme cruelty shown her in life continued in the minutes following her demise. The executioner cut her down, and the guards tossed her body into a makeshift grave (in some accounts a rocky crevice) in the side of the hill. No prayers were said, no marker was placed on the grave, and no one was allowed to stay and pay their respects.

Bridget Bishop is hanged for practicing witchcraft.

A Hysterical Public Outcry

The trial and execution of Bridget Bishop sent a shudder through the Puritan communities of Massachusetts. Certainly the other accused witches languishing in jail now despaired more than ever for their own fortunes. If Bishop had been found guilty and hanged so quickly, would they suffer similarly? Also, a few people in high places were disturbed for different reasons. One of the judges, Nathaniel Saltonstall, thought that the evidence against Bishop had been flimsy; moreover, he felt that the way she was treated on the day of her execution was un-Christian and reprehensible. So he resigned from the court. Jonathan Corwin, who had helped run the pretrial questioning sessions, took his place. In addition, a group of local ministers voiced their concerns about the admission of spectral evidence in the trials. Like Saltonstall, they worried that it was unreliable. But the remaining judges disagreed, and such evidence remained admissible.

The witch trials resumed on June 28. On that day and the two that followed, five women were tried—Sarah Good, Sarah Wilds, Elizabeth Howe, Susannah Martin, and Rebecca Nurse. As had happened during the earlier questioning sessions, Betty Parris, Abigail Williams, and the other supposedly afflicted girls were allowed to be present. And as per usual, they repeatedly threw fits and claimed that the defendants' specters were tormenting them.

Sarah Good became the second person found guilty in the trials, and she went to her death on Gallows Hill on July 19. Right to the end, a local minister, Nicholas Noyes, harassed her and denounced her as an evil witch. At the last moment, the courageous Good stunned the crowd by loudly telling him, "You are a liar. I am no more a witch than you are a wizard, and if you must take

A Juror Explains the Verdict Against Rebecca Nurse

One of the jurors in Rebecca Nurse's trial, Thomas Fisk, later explained why the jury had first found her innocent, then changed the verdict to guilty:

July 4, 1692. I Thomas Fisk . . . being one of them that were of the jury the last week at Salem Court, upon the Trial of Rebecca Nurse, etc., being desired by some of the relations why the jury brought her in guilty after her verdict [of] not guilty; I do hereby give my reasons to be as follows. When the verdict [of] not Guilty was [given], the honored Court was pleased to object against it. After the honored [judges of the] Court had [reminded the jurors about some damning phrases Nurse had uttered in the past], several of the jury declared themselves desirous to go out again, and thereupon the honored Court gave leave. [These phrases, which] were affirmed to have been spoken by her . . . were to me [the] principal evidence against her.

Quoted in *Salem Witchcraft Trials, 1692,* Famous American Trials, "The Trial of Rebecca Nurse." www.law.umkc.edu/faculty/projects/ftrials/salem/ASA_NUR.HTM.

The home of Rebecca Nurse, who was found innocent of being a witch, but was ultimately hanged due to hysterical public outcry.

my life, God will give you blood to drink."[35] According to tradition, this curse was eventually fulfilled. Some local records claim that twenty-five years later, Noyes choked to death on blood released by a bout of internal bleeding.

In the eyes of those present, as well as of posterity, the most remarkable of the five cases tried at the end of June 1692 was that of Rebecca Nurse. Thirty-nine local

residents mustered the nerve to sign a petition in her behalf. One of them was the influential John Putnam (brother of Thomas Putnam), who had earlier denounced Nurse but then changed his mind. The document stated in part: "We never had any cause or grounds to suspect her of any such thing as she is now accused of."[36] The members of the jury found themselves agreeing with the petitioners, as

Nurse presented herself in court as a respectable Christian woman. Thus, the jury initially found her innocent.

However, this verdict was not destined to stand, because too many people had either a vested interest in or a strong expectation of finding all five women guilty. Immediately after the verdict was announced, the afflicted girls went into violent spasms. At the same time, hundreds of onlookers, including those who had earlier denounced and questioned the defendants, cried out in loud voices. Meanwhile, outside the building the news of the verdict caused dozens of people to have fits almost as bad as those of the girls inside.

Seeing all this commotion, the surprised and terrified judges concluded that the jury must have made a mistake. They admonished the jurors to reconsider. And soon Rebecca Nurse's verdict was changed to guilty. At the last moment, Governor Phipps granted her a reprieve. But another hysterical public outcry scared him into recalling it, and Nurse was hanged on July 19 along with Good, Wilds, Howe, and Martin. Hearing of their convictions and deaths, the other prisoners became distraught. It had begun to look as though everyone who had been accused of witchcraft would soon meet similar fates.

Chapter Five

Salem in the Grip of Mass Hysteria

The deaths of Rebecca Nurse, Sarah Good, and three other convicted women on July 19, 1692, were not enough to satisfy the courts, the accusers, and the public that the danger posed by witches in their midst was over. In fact, nothing seemed capable of quelling the rising tide of witchcraft hysteria that now held Salem and surrounding towns in a viselike grip. As the trials and executions continued, it was as if more than merely a few ignorant and spiteful young women had been possessed by evil. Almost the entire community appeared to be in the throes of terror and paranoia that had been manufactured in the minds of its citizens. Even more twisted was the fact that the people as a whole seemed to crave and thrive on the fear and hysteria, as if they were a way to vent human passions that had long been denied open expression. "The nearly universal belief in devils and witches," Marion L. Starkey points out,

could not alone explain the capitulation [surrender] of reason which took place. The fact was that the commonwealth, no less than the girls, craved its [pagan] mysteries. A people whose natural impulses had long been repressed by the severity of their belief, whose security had been undermined by anxiety and terror continued longer than could be borne, demanded their catharsis [emotional release]. Frustrated by the devils they could not reach, they demanded a scapegoat and a full-scale lynching. And they got it.[37]

Under these unfortunate conditions, August and September of 1692 witnessed the height of the madness and the most heinous spilling of innocent people's blood in colonial Salem. Fourteen more guiltless people suffered horrific deaths, and hundreds more were either imprisoned, tortured, or both. Meanwhile,

Procter's Property Seized

Roughly a decade after the conclusion of the Salem witch trials, a Boston merchant named Robert Calef published a synopsis of the trials titled More Wonders of the Invisible World. *In this passage, he tells about the seizure of John Procter's property by the authorities:*

John Procter and his wife being in prison, the sheriff came to his house and seized all the goods, provisions, and cattle that he could come at [find], and sold some of the cattle at half price, and killed others, and put them up [for sale in] the West Indies. [They] threw out the beer out of a barrel and carried away the barrel; emptied a pot of broth and took away the pot, and left nothing in the house for the support of the children. No part of the said goods are known to be returned.

Quoted in Piney.com, "Robert Calef, *More Wonders of the Invisible World.*" www.piney.com/ColCalef1.html.

some of those who managed to survive were cruelly stripped of their belongings and forced into a life of beggary. During these two months of what might be described as societal insanity, the authorities largely ignored a number of petitions and other pleas for the return of reason and justice.

On Deaf Ears

One such plea had been lodged by Rebecca Nurse shortly before her execution. After her jury had been coerced to reconsider its verdict of innocence, she had been recalled to the courtroom to clarify some earlier testimony. At that time a juror asked her a question. But because she was partly deaf, as well as old, ill, and distraught, she did not hear it and remained silent. Only later was she told that she had been asked the ques-

tion and had failed to answer it, thereby sealing her fate. She therefore wrote an appeal to the court, explaining that she had simply not heard the question. But the judges, like almost everyone else in Salem, were too swept up in the wave of public hysteria to give this appeal for fair treatment and mercy any credence.

Four days after Nurse was hanged on Gallows Hill, John Procter, still in his jail cell, penned a longer, more moving plea. It was addressed to Increase Mather and four other prominent local ministers. Evidently, Procter hoped that these supposedly learned and godly men would somehow transcend the existing paranoid atmosphere and use their influence to stop the trials. "Nothing but our innocent blood will serve" those who had accused him and his cellmates of witchcraft, he wrote. The judges had "condemned us already before our trials," Procter complained, something manifestly unfair. Therefore, he and his fellow inmates "beg and implore your favorable assistance of this our humble petition . . . that if it be possible our innocent blood may be spared."[38]

In the same letter, Procter exposed another grossly unjust and brutal tactic employed by the authorities in their zeal to root out and destroy witches. He pointed out that much of the so-called evidence against him and the others had been provided by five other suspected witches who had given said evidence under duress. In particular, at least two of these individuals had been tortured. They "would not confess anything," Procter said, "till they tied them neck and heels till the blood was ready to come out of their noses."[39] The "neck and heels" torture consisted of looping a rope around a person's neck and then tying it to his or her ankles; this caused extreme discomfort, pain, and often nosebleeds.

Unfortunately for Procter, his petition for justice and fair treatment fell mostly on deaf ears. The same was true of a petition submitted to the authorities on behalf of Elizabeth Procter and her husband by thirty-one of their friends and neighbors. It read in part: "God may permit Satan to impersonate, dissemble, and thereby abuse innocents. . . . As to what we have ever seen of [Elizabeth and John Procter], upon our consciences we judge them innocent of the crime objected."[40]

The petitioners had brought up a point that had been debated by many in the colony in recent weeks. They held that the devil, with his evil cunning, could make an innocent person look guilty. In contrast, many other Puritans believed that only guilty people succumbed to the wiles of the devil; therefore, Elizabeth and John Procter must be guilty.

The Power of Darkness

It was this second view that prevailed when the Procters went to trial on August 5, 1692. In fact, the proceedings went swiftly and in essence did no more than confirm the findings of the Procters' memorable questioning session on April 11. As in all the hearings and trials, much of the testimony and evidence against the defendants had come from the afflicted girls, who were ever-present in the room. In addition, Tituba's husband, John Indian, had been present that day. He had initiated a commotion that had quickly turned into an uproar. Right after Mrs. Procter took the stand, he shouted, "There is the woman who came in her shift [spectral form] and choked me!"[41] Hearing that, the girls began moaning and twitching. Some of them claimed that the defendant's specter was at that moment crouched on one of the courtroom's ceiling beams. That revelation quite naturally caused a wave of fear to sweep over the spectators in the chamber.

Amid the girls' groans and cries and the mounting clamor coming from the onlookers in the room, the Procters tried to inject the proverbial voice of reason into the proceedings. Elizabeth Procter charitably attempted to calm Abigail Williams, who had just denounced her. Meanwhile, John Procter ran to his wife's side as if to defend

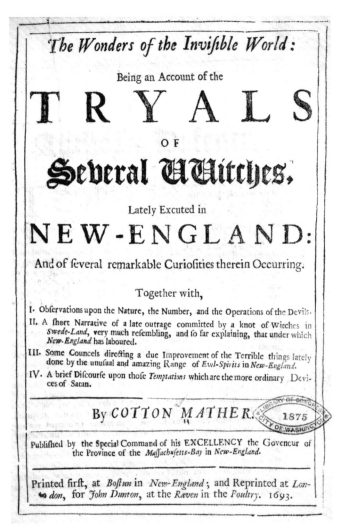

Cotton Mather penned a book on witchcraft, The Wonders of the Invisible World: Being an Account of the Tryals of Several Witches.

the prosecutors lashed out at John Procter, saying: "You see, the devil will deceive you! The children could see what you were going to do before [you did it]. I would advise you to repent, for the devil is bringing you out [exposing you]."[43]

Procter, a strong, assertive, outspoken individual, must have been crestfallen and deeply disturbed that the court would take the word of some hysterical, untrustworthy children over his. But the reality of the trials was that the magistrates and judges had been thoroughly drawn into the eerie, twisted, invisible world the girls had manufactured. As Starkey puts it:

The common sense of these men had abdicated before the crazed fantasies of wenches in their teens.... Procter's reasoning was like blasphemy to the magistrates. With them, the devil had indeed taken over. This was his hour and [also the hour of] the power of darkness.... It was a logic that admitted only one reality, the affliction of these girls and their testimony as to its cause.[44]

her. Seeing him, Abigail shouted out, "Why, he can pinch as well as she!"[42] The implication was that the man's specter had begun to harass the girls, which sent the spectators into a tumult.

When the judges finally managed to restore order, it was already too late for the Procters. The damage had been done, and any hopes they had had that they would be able to use reason and common sense to reverse the course of the witchcraft hysteria had been dashed. One of

Thus, when the Procters entered the courtroom on August 5, the two were already guilty in the judges' eyes. The latter pronounced the expected verdict and sentenced the two to death. However, Elizabeth Procter was pregnant at the time, so she was given a temporary reprieve until her baby was born, after which she was to be hanged. John Procter went to his death on Gallows Hill on August 19. Either shortly before or after his untimely demise, the local authorities seized all his properties and belongings. One of the magistrates seized his cattle, sold some at half their market value, and slaughtered the rest for sale to the West Indies. The house and barn were stripped of everything, even storage barrels and pots and pans.

The "Queen of Hell"

The Procters were not the only people tried on August 5, 1692. Martha Carrier, a resident of the town of Andover, and George Jacobs Sr., a seventy-year-old grandfather who needed two canes to walk, also faced the judges and jury. Much of the evidence against Carrier was provided by neighbors

George Jacobs was put on trial for practicing witchcraft in 1692.

who had had property disputes with her. Typical was the testimony of Benjamin and Sarah Abbot. They claimed that they had argued with Martha Carrier about the proper placement of a boundary running between their two farms and that Carrier had lost her temper and threatened to get back at Benjamin Abbot. In his testimony, Abbot listed the afflictions supposedly caused by Carrier in her efforts to seek revenge:

> Presently after [the dispute] I was taken with a swelling in my foot and then was taken with a pain in my side . . . which bred to a sore which was lanced by Docter Prescott. . . . Then one other sore did breed in my groin which was lanced by Doctor Prescott also . . . and put me to very great misery, so that it brought me almost to death's door and continued until Goodwife Carrier was taken . . . by the constable, and that very day I begun to grow better. . . . Ever since, [I] have [had] great cause to think that the [Goodwife] Carrier had a great hand in my sickness and misery [by practicing witchcraft].[45]

In addition to supposed evidence of this nature, Martha Carrier was condemned on the accusations of several people who confirmed that she was a witch. These included her own sons, who were severely tortured in jail to force them to denounce their mother. Amid the presentation of all this trumped-up evidence, Carrier remained defiant, calling

the witnesses and afflicted girls liars and the whole proceedings shameful. This annoyed and in some cases enraged the community's authority figures, including Cotton Mather, who later called her "the rampant hag" who wanted to become "Queen of Hell."[46]

As for George Jacobs, one of the afflicted girls, Sarah Churchill, and a local boy, John DeRich, claimed that the old man's specter had chased or beaten them. Jacobs realized that he had no way of refuting such fantastic accusations and seemed resigned to his fate. He is credited with telling the magistrates, "Well, burn me or hang me. I will stand in the truth of Jesus Christ!"[47] The judges proceeded to oblige him by sentencing him to death. Jacobs and Martha Carrier were both hanged on August 19 along with John Procter. Afterward, the authorities went to Jacobs's home and confiscated everything, including his wife's wedding ring. Old Mrs. Jacobs had to spend the last of her money to buy back her clothes from the sheriff; consequently, she thereafter had no means of support and had to beg for scraps of food to sustain herself in her last, misery-filled years.

The Leader of the Witches?

Still another person who lost his life on Gallows Hill on August 19 was the Reverend George Burroughs. His case demonstrated that the witchcraft hysteria in the colony had grown to such proportions that even Puritan ministers were not safe. His trial was seen as particularly important because several people had accused him of being the evil leader of all the

George Burroughs stands trial in Salem, Massachusetts, in 1692.

witches that had been afflicting the colony. Thus, a number of prominent members of the community attended Burroughs's trial, including noted ministers Increase Mather, Deodat Lawson, and John Hale.

The testimony against Burroughs was vivid, lurid, and damning. Because he was an unusually muscular and strong man, witnesses claimed that his strength must have come from the devil. He was also accused of biting numerous people while in spectral form. One of the afflicted girls, Ann Putnam, gave a deposition that stated in part:

On the 20th of April, 1692, at evening [I] saw the apparition [specter] of a minister at which [I] was grievously affrighted and cried out. . . . [I asked] "Whence came you, and what is your name, for I will complain of you . . . if you be a wizard." And immediately I was tortured by him, being racked [stretched] and almost choked by him, and he tempted me to write in his [evil devil's] book, which I refused with loud outcries. . . . Then presently he told me that his name was George Burroughs and that he had had three wives and that he had bewitched the first two of them to death.[48]

During the trial, which lasted only a couple of hours at best, Burroughs seemed rattled, despondent, even lost in thought. Perhaps he was in a state of shock over being accused of such heinous crimes. He knew full well that he was innocent. And it is possible that

Mercy Lewis Denounces the Reverend Burroughs

Among the many incriminating statements made against the Reverend George Burroughs during his trial was that of the afflicted girl Mercy Lewis:

On the 7th of May 1692, at evening I saw the apparition of Mr. George Burroughs whom I very well knew, which did grievously torture me and urged me to write in his [evil devil's] book. . . . He told me that he . . . had bewitched Mr. Shepherd's daughter, and that . . . the devil was his servant. . . . Then he again tortured me most dreadfully and threatened to kill me, for he said that I should not [bear] witness against him. Also, he told me that he had made Abigail Hobbs a witch and several more [young women witches]. Then again he did most dreadfully torture me.

Quoted in Frances Hill, ed., *The Salem Witch Trials Reader*. New York: Da Capo, 2000, p. 197.

he was in a paralyzing quandary, wondering why God would allow him, a devoted minister, to suffer such lies and indignities. Whatever the reason for Burroughs's silence on the stand, it made him seem all the more guilty to the judges, jury, and onlookers. No one was surprised when he was found guilty and sentenced to be hanged.

To Burroughs's everlasting credit, however, his presence of mind returned to him as he approached the hanging tree. A few seconds after he climbed the ladder beneath the noose, he turned to the assembled crowd and loudly proclaimed his innocence. Then he did a brilliant thing by reciting the Lord's Prayer in moving tones and without making a single mistake. Puritan society and law held that a witch or other evil being was incapable of doing this, so a hush suddenly fell over the crowd; many people who a few moments before had taunted and jeered the minister now found themselves doubting his guilt. Seeing this unexpected turn of events, the authorities speedily hung Burroughs before he could rally any more support. They then buried him so hastily that, according to some accounts, his chin and hand remained protruding from the ground.

"More Weight"

Not all of the people tried for witchcraft and sentenced to die were executed by hanging, as Burroughs, Carrier, Jacobs, and Procter were in August. In September, Giles Corey, a farmer in his eighties, suffered a considerably slower demise.

Corey had testified against his own wife, Martha, in March, in large part because he did not grasp the gravity of the situation at the time. Later, in April, several of the afflicted girls accused the old man himself, saying that his specter had tormented them. When questioned, Corey had insisted: "I never did hurt them."[49]

Evidently Corey remained incredulous that he would actually be brought to trial for witchcraft. But when he realized that his trial was indeed imminent, he began to worry what would happen to his property if he was convicted. Ignorant of the law, he decided that his best strategy was to clam up and say nothing further. Corey even refused to plead either guilty or not guilty before the court.

The authorities had very seldom encountered such stubbornness by someone accused of a crime. So they tried to get Corey to enter a plea by submitting him to a torture called pien-fort-et-dure (French for "a punishment hard and severe"), an old European method of obtaining confessions. It was also called pressing, because it consisted of making the victim lie face-up on the ground, placing a board on his or her chest, and then loading large rocks onto the board. Thus, a great deal of weight pressed down on the person, eventually cracking the ribs and crushing the lungs.

When Corey refused to speak, the authorities took him to a field near the courthouse and began pressing him while a crowd of onlookers watched. They hoped that at some point the slow suffocation caused by the increasing

After Giles Corey refused to plead either guilty or not guilty to being a witch, he was subjected to torture in order to obtain a confession.

weight would convince the old man to give in and cooperate. But during the entire affair he uttered only two words: "More weight."[50] In this way, Giles Corey had the breath and life crushed out of him on September 19, 1692.

Thankfully, Corey's case marked the only instance in the history of the Massachusetts Bay Colony in which pressing was employed. But that did not make the old man's surviving relatives feel any better. In fact, the entire incident had a sort of unsettling effect on much of the populace. Like the Reverend Burroughs's recital of the Lord's Prayer on Gallows Hill, the cruel killing of Giles Corey made many Puritans wonder if justice was truly being served in the ongoing witch hunt and trials.

To help keep that hunt from losing steam, one of the parties with a strong stake in it, Thomas Putnam, quickly presented

Giles Corey Is Questioned

Part of the questioning session of eighty-year-old Giles Corey on April 19, 1692, is excerpted here:

Corey: I never did hurt them [the afflicted girls].

Magistrate: It is your appearance [that] hurts them, they charge you. Tell us what you have done.

Corey: I have done nothing to damage them.

Magistrate: Have you never entered into contract with the devil?

Corey: I never did.

Magistrate: What temptations have you had?

Corey: I never had temptations in my life. . . .

Magistrate: What was it [that] frightened you in the barn?

Corey: I know nothing that frightened me there.

Magistrate: Why, here are three witnesses that heard you say so today.

Corey: I do not remember it.

Quoted in Marilynne K. Roach, *The Salem Witch Trials: A Day-by-Day Chronicle of a Community Under Siege.* New York: Taylor Trade, 2002, pp. 77–78.

Tourists who come to Salem can visit sites such as the Witch House.

new evidence to one of the judges. According to Putnam, on the day of Corey's death a large group of invisible witches tried to press his daughter, Ann, to death. Then the girl had been visited by a friendly spirit, which told her that Corey's death was deserved and that because of it Ann would be spared.

Though this story, clearly manufactured by the elder Putnam, soothed some members of the community, others were not convinced. Cracks were beginning to form in the wall of hysteria that had cut Salem off from the world of reason, justice, and mercy. And soon, that deadly edifice would collapse completely.

Chapter Six

Too Many Witches: The Trials End

Giles Corey was not the only Puritan who was executed in September 1692. On September 9, six people were tried for witchcraft, convicted, and sentenced to hang. They included Mary Esty, Alice Parker, Martha Corey (Giles Corey's wife), Dorcas Hoar, Mary Bradbury, and Ann Pudeator. Then, on September 17, nine more suspects were tried and sentenced to die: Wilmot Redd, Mary Parker, Margaret Scott, Samuel Wardwell, Abigail Falkner, Mary Lacey, Rebecca Eames, Anne Foster, and Abigail Hobbs. Of these fifteen condemned people, eight were executed on Gallows Hill on September 22. The others were spared for various reasons. Abigail Falkner, for example, like Elizabeth Procter the month before, received a temporary reprieve because she was carrying a child. Dorcas Hoar escaped death by accusing others of witchcraft. And Mary Bradbury may have eluded her own execution by bribing her jailers.

Yet even as the eight met their deaths on September 22, the witch trials were, unbeknownst to all involved at the time, nearing an abrupt end. The toxic atmosphere in Salem was beginning to dissipate. This was partly because of incidents such as the Reverend Burroughs's display of purity on Gallows Hill and Giles Corey's show of courage and personal conviction as he was pressed to death. A number of people in the community had come to doubt that these men actually had been guilty of witchcraft.

The changing atmosphere in the community was also fueled by the doubts and concerns of a few prominent, educated, and highly respected citizens who began to see the hysteria for what it was. Particularly influential in this regard was Thomas Brattle, by far the most educated person in New England's Puritan society. Brattle was a college graduate, a world renowned astronomer and mathematician, and a member of England's

A modern-day tourist walks up Gallows Hill, where many accused witches were put to death.

prestigious scientific organization, the Royal Society. On October 8, only sixteen days after the most recent executions, he boldly suggested that most or all of the supernatural visions experienced by the afflicted girls were figments of their imaginations. "Many of these afflicted persons," he wrote,

who have scores of strange fits in a day, yet in the intervals of time [in between] are hale and hearty, robust and lusty, as though nothing had afflicted them. . . . Furthermore, these afflicted persons do say . . . that they can see specters when their eyes are shut. . . . I am sure they lie, [or] at least speak falsely . . . for [this] is an utter impossibility. It is true, they may strongly fancy, or have things represented in their imaginations when their eyes are shut. And I think this is all that ought to be allowed to these blind, nonsensical girls.[51]

Simply put, as the truth and reliability of the evidence given by the afflicted girls increasingly came into question, the foundations of the witchcraft hysteria started to crumble, and the trials could not go on.

Supporting the Innocence of Those Executed

In his long public statement released on October 8, 1692, the noted English intellectual Thomas Brattle disputed the evidence presented in the witch trials and suggested that the accusations of the afflicted girls could not be trusted. He also pointed out, in this passage, that many of the executed persons seemed innocent when facing their deaths:

In the opinion of many unprejudiced, considerate, and considerable spectators, some of the condemned went out of the world not only with great protestations, but also with good shows of innocency. . . . They protested their innocency as in the presence of the great God, whom forthwith they were to appear before. They wished . . . that their blood might be the last innocent blood shed upon that account. With great affection [emotion], they entreated Mr. Cotton Mather to pray with them. They prayed that God would discover what witchcrafts were among us. They forgave their accusers. . . . They prayed earnestly for pardon for all other sins . . . and [they] seemed to be very sincere, upright, and sensible of their circumstances.

Quoted in Frances Hill, ed., *The Salem Witch Trials Reader*. New York: Da Capo, 2000, pp. 91–92.

Two Fundamental Mistakes

Brattle found that he was not alone in holding suspect the honesty and integrity of the girls' accusations and testimony. Said accusations continued after the September 22 hangings, increasing both in number and outrageousness. The number of those accused by Abigail Williams rose to at least 40. Meanwhile, an accused witch claimed she had attended a meeting involving some 200 witches, and someone else said that there were more than 500 witches in the colony. In the midst of the hysteria, an Andover man, William Barker, reported that Satan was planning to destroy all the churches in Massachusetts and replace worship of God with worship of the devil. By about October 1, 1692, some 150 accused witches were rotting in colonial jails, and at least another 200 had been accused of witchcraft but were not yet arrested because there was no more room in those jails.

It was not simply the numbers of suspected witches that had begun to strain believability. It was also who was being accused. Throughout most of the witch hunt, hearings, and trials, the vast majority of suspects had been poor, or at least of modest means, and also socially and politically powerless. But in late September and early October, the afflicted girls began accusing people of much higher standing in the community. The mother-in-law of magistrate Jonathan Corwin was accused of being a witch, for instance. Also accused were the two sons of a well-respected former governor, Simon Bradstreet, and the wife of the Reverend John Hale, one of the most distinguished churchmen in New England. Finally, Lady Phipps, wife of the present governor, William Phipps, was publicly accused of practicing witchcraft. It is revealing that none of these people were arrested, nor were the accusations against them taken seriously, even for a moment. Clearly, the supposedly afflicted girls had finally gone too far.

In retrospect, modern observers have pointed out that the girls and other accusers had made two fundamental mistakes. First, there were simply too many witches. It was one thing to accuse a few members of society of being evil agents of the devil; it was quite another to claim that the colony was literally riddled with hundreds or thousands of witches. Even the most gullible and religiously devout members of the community began to see that such claims had to be excessive and therefore that the accusers themselves could not be trusted.

Second, in their youthful ignorance, vanity, and frenzied attempt to exert power over their society, the girls eventually thought they could bring down the rich and powerful folk who ran that society. But this was self-delusion. As has been true time after time in history, those in the corridors of power could not be easily dislodged from their high positions. As soon as they and their families were threatened by the widening hysteria, the trials suddenly came to a proverbial grinding halt. On October 12, 1692, Governor Phipps ordered that all imprisonment of people on suspicion of witchcraft must immediately cease. And a few

In 1692, while William Phipps (pictured) was serving as governor of Massachusetts, his wife was accused of being a witch.

weeks later, on October 29, he officially shut down the court of Oyer and Terminer. The Salem witch trials were, for all intents and purposes, over.

Eliminating a "Delusion of the Devil"

But though the witchcraft trials had ended, the local jails were still full of people who had been accused of evil doings.

The quandary the governor and other community leaders now faced was what to do with these prisoners. At first, the officials were reluctant simply to release them all. After all, what if some of them were indeed witches? The fact that the afflicted girls had gone too far by accusing Lady Phipps of being a witch did not necessarily indicate that all of the earlier accusations had been wrong.

Too Many Witches: The Trials End ■ 83

The solution seemed to be to create a new court. Its mandate would be not to try new witches, but to decide which of the prisoners could safely be released and which should remain in custody. The expectation was that the new court would be much fairer than the earlier one because no spectral evidence would be allowed. Indeed, without the girls' testimony that they saw invisible beings harassing them and others, little other convincing evidence of witchcraft remained. So when thirty of the prisoners were tried by the new court on January 3, 1693, twenty-seven had their cases speedily dismissed. The other three persons were found guilty, mainly because they had confessed to being witches.

Though by law the three convicted people were subject to the death penalty, they were never executed. Governor Phipps granted them pardons, saying, "Considering how the matter had been [so badly] managed [in the previous trials], I sent a reprieve, whereby the execution was stopped." Furthermore, Phipps stated that he wanted to eliminate

The Salem Witchcraft Trial Memorial, which was dedicated in 1992.

the black cloud that threatened this province with destruction. For . . . this delusion of the devil did spread and its effects touched the lives and estates of many of their Majesty's subjects and [the] reputations of some of the principal persons here, and indeed unhappily clogged and interrupted their Majesty's affairs, which has been a great vexation to me.[52]

Trying to put the colony's troubles in the past and restore a semblance of order and justice, in May 1693 Phipps granted pardons to all those still held in the jails. Even those who had escaped confinement by fleeing the colony were pardoned. This meant that the fugitives could safely come home and that the authorities could begin freeing those who were languishing behind bars.

In Search of Justice

In spite of the governor's pardons, however, emptying the prisons was not a simple matter. This is because under the colony's laws prisoners were financially responsible for their own upkeep while confined in jail. So only those who could afford it, or whose relatives could afford it, could obtain release. "Criminals were not coddled in these days," Marion L. Starkey explains,

nor were those on whom the merest shadow of suspicion had ever rested. You did not in prison become the guest of the state. [Instead] you paid your way. Even

if you were wholly innocent, if it were proved that you had been wrongly deprived of your liberty, you still could not leave until you had reimbursed the jailer for his expenditures in your behalf, the food he had fed you, the shackles he had placed on your wrists and ankles. Prices varied slightly at the various prisons, but in general board averaged about two shillings and sixpence a week. Some of the witches had been running up a bill at this rate for more than a year. . . . Farms had to be mortgaged to raise the ransom, and they were often farms already impoverished by the half-hearted attention they had had while the trials monopolized everyone's time and attention.[53]

As a result of these unpleasant realities, some people were forced to remain in jail well after they had been pardoned. A few, including an elderly woman named Sarah Daston, wasted away and died in captivity, abandoned to their sad fate by family, friends, and society. Inmate Mary Watkins managed to get out only after a Virginia planter paid her prison bills in exchange for her working for several years as his indentured servant. Meanwhile, another imprisoned woman, Margaret Jacobs, had the good fortune to have a kindly local citizen pay her way to freedom; she was expected to pay him back, but only at a rate that she could manage comfortably. The two pregnant women convicted of being witches, Elizabeth Procter and Abigail

Falkner, were not so lucky. They had their babies in jail. And when they finally got out, they were scorned by most people and experienced both social rejection and poverty for many years to come.

Thus, though the trials ended and the prisons eventually emptied, justice was not immediately served in the cases of most who had been drawn into the nightmare of witchcraft hysteria. Yet that did not stop many of these wronged people from seeking justice, even when it took years to achieve it. In 1693, not long after Governor Phipps issued his pardons, several of the released prisoners applied to the colonial government for restitution of their confiscated property. These petitions were summarily ignored. But the injured parties persisted. In 1702, many of their number submitted a petition calling for the legal reversal of all convictions in the witch trials, including those of the people who had been executed. In response, the government passed a bill banning the use of spectral evidence in all future trials in the colony; but no pardons were forthcoming. Finally, in October 1710, a new generation of legislators in Massachusetts saw fit to redress the petitioners. A bill passed reversing all the former convictions. And the government paid financial restitution to the families of twenty-four of the victims.

Humbled in the Dust

In this way, at least a few of the wrongs suffered by the victims of the trials were eventually righted. But what about justice for those who had perpetrated the hysteria and the carnage and misery it had created? With much disdain and anger, many of the victims and their families remembered the key roles played by Rev. Parris, who had stirred up much of the hysteria through his incendiary sermons warning that witches lurked at every turn; by the judges who had so gullibly taken the word of hysterical, attention-seeking children over that of responsible adults with unblemished reputations; and by those very children, the girls who had started all the trouble in the first place. It seemed only fair that these individuals should have to pay some kind of price for their failings.

In at least some cases, the key perpetrators did suffer some kind of negative consequences. In the months following the end of the trials, for instance, Rev. Parris encountered the wrath of many in his congregation who held him partly responsible for the witch hunt. Early in 1693, a group of these Salem Village worshippers attempted to void his salary. "His believing the devil's accusations," they said, "and readily departing from all charity to persecute the blameless and godly [citizens] are just causes for our refusal [to pay him]."[54] Parris fought back for a while. But over time, more and more villagers refused to set foot in church while he was still the minister. So in 1697, he finally resigned and left town, taking young Betty with him. The new village minister, Joseph Green, eventually amended the church's rolls, posthumously reinstating Rebecca Nurse, Giles Corey, and others whom Parris had expelled at the height of witchcraft hysteria.

A Petition for Financial Restitution

Among the petitions for financial restitution brought before the Massachusetts government in 1710 was this one, by Isaac Esty, husband of one of the accused witches, Mary Esty:

Isaac Esty of Topsfield in the county of Essex . . . having been sorely [treated] through the holy and awful providence of God depriving him of his beloved wife Mary Esty, who suffered death in the year 1692 and under the fearful odium of one of the worst of crimes that can be laid to the charge of mankind, as if she had been guilty of witchcraft . . . am firmly persuaded that she was innocent. . . . Upon consideration of a notification from the Honored General Court, desiring myself and others under the like circumstances to give some account of [how much] my estate was [financially damaged] by reason of such a hellish molestation, [I] do hereby declare . . . that my wife was near upon 5 months imprisoned, all which time I provided maintenance for her at my own cost and charge, went constantly twice a week to provide for her what she needed . . . and I was constrained to be at the charge of transporting her to and fro. So that I can not but think my charge in time and money might amount to 20 pounds besides my trouble and sorrow of heart in being deprived of her after such a manner which this world can never make me any compensation for.

Quoted in *Salem Witchcraft Trials, 1692,* Famous American Trials, "Petitions for Compensation and Decision Concerning Compensation, 1710–1711." www.law.umkc.edu/faculty/projects/ftrials/salem/ SAL_PET.HTM.

Most of the judges who had served in the court of Oyer and Terminer did not suffer the kind of social rejection that Rev. Parris did. However, one of their number, Samuel Sewall, did end up atoning for his role in the fiasco. In January 1697, Sewall released a statement that a local minister recited from the pulpit. Amounting to a confession of guilt, it read in part:

As to the guilt contracted upon the opening of the late commission [court] of Oyer and Terminer in Salem, [I, Samuel Sewall] desire to take the blame and shame of it, asking pardon of men, and especially desiring prayers that God . . . would pardon that sin and all [my] other sins.[55]

As for the young girls whose secret play in white magic, fits, and incriminating accusations had largely driven the witch hunt, most were never punished for causing such misery. A few, including Betty Parris, Mercy Lewis, and Mary

Walcott, did eventually marry, although little is known about their later lives. Only one of the girls, Ann Putnam, ever publicly expressed remorse for what she had done. (Betty Parris may have, too, but if so her confession did not survive.) In 1706, Ann penned a confession and gave it to Rev. Green to read to his congregation in Salem Village. "I desire to be humbled before God," it began,

for that sad and humbling providence that befell my father's family in the year about '92 [i.e., 1692]; that I, then being in my childhood, should, by such a providence of God, be made an instrument for the accusing of several persons of a grievous crime, whereby their lives were taken away from them, whom now I have just grounds and good reason to believe they were innocent persons; and that it was a great delusion of Satan that deceived me in that sad time, whereby I justly fear I have been instrumental, with others, though ignorantly and unwittingly, to bring upon myself and this land the guilt of innocent blood. . . . Particularly, as I was a chief instrument of accusing of Goodwife Nurse and her two sisters, I desire to lie in the dust, and to be humbled for it, in that I was a cause, with others, of so sad a calamity to them and their families; for which . . . [I] earnestly beg forgiveness of God, and from all those

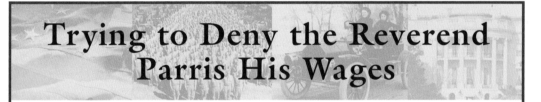

Trying to Deny the Reverend Parris His Wages

In April 1693 several angry members of the Reverend Samuel Parris's congregation, viewing him as an instigator of the shameful witch hunt, went to court to try to stop payment of his salary. The petition is excerpted here:

The said [Reverend] Parris [had been] teaching such dangerous errors and preached such scandalous immoralities as ought to discharge him . . . from the work of the minister. . . . He was equally guilty of perjury with them that swear to what is false. . . . His believing the devil's accusations and readily departing from all charity to prosecute the blameless and godly [citizens] are just causes for our refusal [to pay him]. . . . [Mr. Parris] has been the beginner and procurer of the sorest affliction, not to the village only, but to the whole country [i.e., colony].

Quoted in Marion L. Starkey, *The Devil in Massachusetts: A Modern Enquiry into the Salem Witch Trials.* New York: Random House, 1989, p. 250.

unto whom I have given just cause of sorrow and offence.[56]

No one knows, of course, whether God ever forgave Ann Putnam and the other girls. For their part, the members of Rev. Green's flock generously forgave her and allowed her to join them. But there were many in Salem, including some who had lived through the witch hunt and their children born later, who refused to accept such apologies after the fact. In their view, repentance, though admirable, could not bring back dead loved ones or restore ruined family reputations.

Typical of those who held grudges all their lives was Philip English, a Salem merchant whose wife, Mary, had been accused of witchcraft, rudely dragged from her bed, and thrown into jail. (She was later released.) For decades following the trials, English loudly denounced all the former authority figures who had run them, including the Reverend Nicholas Noyes. On several occasions over the years, English was arrested for slander and spent the night in jail. But his anger over the treatment of his wife and the brutal, untimely deaths of his friends John Procter and Rebecca Nurse never subsided. On his deathbed in 1736, English was urged finally to forgive Noyes, who had died several years before. Among English's last words were "I'll be damned if I forgive him!"[57]

Epilogue

The Popular Legacy of the Trials

The Salem witch trials had both short-term and long-term legacies. In the short term, the witch hysteria, convictions, imprisonments, and executions showed the English settlers of North America what could happen if they allowed their worst fears and darkest urges to get the better of them. And this had the beneficial effect of making colonial society more tolerant and its legal system more fair. In the decades following the trials, people everywhere realized that these proceedings had been a travesty of justice. No one wanted something similar to be repeated. So laws were passed to ban spectral and other questionable evidence from colonial courtrooms. Over time, this contributed to the ongoing legal and political reforms that laid the groundwork for the reasoned and equitable justice system adopted by the infant United States in the late 1700s.

Tourism Proves Inevitable

A more long-term legacy of the Salem witch trials was the permanent association of the town of Salem with witches and witchcraft. In the generation or two following the trials, most local residents wanted only to forget about them. They certainly did not want outsiders to come and gawk at houses, churches, and other Salem landmarks associated with the trials and their participants. But later generations came to realize that this was inevitable. And the inhabitants of the area learned that they could profit from a tourist trade driven by curiosity about the trials and executions of witches in colonial times.

Indeed, as early as the 1830s, visitors began to come from surrounding towns and states to scale Gallows Hill and relive, at least in their imaginations, the horrors that had taken place there. By about 1870, the first products manufac-

Salem's East Church, which houses the Salem Witch Museum, is now a tourist attraction.

tured especially for tourists went on sale in Salem. The earliest souvenirs were pebbles bearing paintings of witches flying on brooms; soon afterward, silverware, dinner plates, tea strainers, jewelry, and other items stamped with the images of witches were enjoying brisk sales.

The witch logo proved popular and durable. Today, Salem's police and fire departments use it, as does the local paper, the *Salem Evening Post*. In addition, the mascot of the Salem High School football team is a witch. Modern Salem also features several witch-related museums,

tours, and haunted house attractions, the latter mainly during the Halloween season. Tourists also flock to the Salem Witchcraft Trial Memorial, dedicated in 1992 to mark the three hundredth anniversary of the infamous trials.

Fighting the Furies of Fanaticism

Among the honored guests attending the dedication ceremony that year was the great American playwright Arthur Miller. It was particularly appropriate that Miller should be there, because he

A scene from the 1996 film version of Arthur Miller's The Crucible.

was the author of the most famous work of literature ever written about the Salem trials. Composed in 1952, his play, *The Crucible,* swiftly became a sensation and remains a modern theatrical classic.

The manner in which Miller treated the witch trials and his motivation for writing the play highlighted perhaps the most important legacy of the Salem witch hysteria. Namely, the play serves as a parable, a lesson, and a warning for people in all times and places. At the time that Miller penned the play, the McCarthy hearings were in full swing. In what amounted to little more than a modern witch hunt, U.S. senator Joseph McCarthy of Wisconsin chaired hearings by the House Committee on Un-American Activities (HUAC). He and his cronies were eager to root out Communists and Communist sympathizers, whom they suspected lurked everywhere in American society. In his excessive zeal, McCarthy stirred up the same kind of social hysteria and utilized some of the same unfair tactics that had made the Salem trials possible. The lives of many people, most of whom had little or no connection to Communist causes, were ruined.

Eventually, McCarthy's witch hunt collapsed for the same reason that the Salem trials ended. A majority of fair-minded people in society saw through the hysteria and demanded an end to it and the injustices it had brought about. *The Crucible* contributed to opening people's eyes and making them think about what was happening in their own country. Miller's play showed, and still shows, that there is a very real tendency for people everywhere to allow their darker urges to surface and run rampant. Commenting in 1996 about this still frequently staged play, Miller said:

Playwright Arthur Miller's work about the witch trials, The Crucible, *also targeted the "witch hunts" of the McCarthy era.*

"The Crucible" starts getting produced wherever a political coup appears imminent, or a dictatorial regime has just been overthrown. From Argentina to Chile to Greece, Czechoslovakia, China, and a dozen other places, the play seems to present the same primeval structure of human sacrifice to the furies of fanaticism and paranoia that goes on repeating itself forever, as though imbedded in the brain of social man.[58]

Miller, who died in 2005, recognized that the key to keeping such paranoia from surfacing in the future is understanding. That is why his play, along with films and history books about the Salem witch trials, are still vitally important. They educate people about the horrors of the past, while reminding them that they, too, are only human and could, under the right circumstances, be drawn into the next witch hunt. As Frances Hill so aptly phrases it:

> The tendency for witch hunts to start, and continue, is exacerbated [made worse] by a society's or group's insistence on its monopoly of righteousness. The counter-tendency [i.e., the effort to keep such witch hunts from occurring in the first place] is promoted by an understanding and acceptance of the fallibility of all human beings, including ourselves.[59]

Notes

Introduction: Down the Dark Paths of Fear and Hatred

1. Frances Hill, ed., *The Salem Witch Trials Reader.* New York: Da Capo, 2000, p. xvii.
2. Quoted in *The Malleus Maleficarum of James Sprenger and Heinrich Kramer,* "The *Malleus Maleficarum,* Part I." www.malleusmaleficarum.org/part_I/mm01_06a.html.
3. James A. Haught, *Holy Horrors.* New York: Prometheus, 1990, pp. 75–76.
4. Haught, *Holy Horrors,* p. 76.
5. Hill, *The Salem Witch Trials Reader,* p. 3.

Chapter One: Salem on the Eve of the Witch Trials

6. Marilynne K. Roach, *The Salem Witch Trials: A Day-by-Day Chronicle of a Community Under Siege.* New York: Taylor Trade, 2002, p. xix.
7. Richard Weisman, *Witchcraft, Magic, and Religion in 17th-Century Massachusetts.* Amherst: University of Massachusetts Press, 1984, p. 26.
8. Marion L. Starkey, *The Devil in Massachusetts: A Modern Enquiry into the Salem Witch Trials.* New York: Random House, 1989, p. 31.
9. Starkey, *The Devil in Massachusetts,* p. 32.
10. Carol F. Karlsen, *The Devil in the Shape of a Woman: Witchcraft in Colonial New England.* Magnolia, MA: Peter Smith, 1999, p. 46.
11. Quoted in Hill, *The Salem Witch Trials Reader,* p. 126.

Chapter Two: Strange Behaviors Diagnosed as Witchcraft

12. Quoted in Hanover Historical Texts Projects, "Increase Mather: *Remarkable Providences: An Essay for the Recording of Illustrious Providences* (Boston, 1684)." http://history.hanover.edu/texts/matherrp.html.
13. Quoted in Hanover Historical Texts Projects, "Increase Mather."
14. Quoted in Hill, *The Salem Witch Trials Reader,* p. 19.
15. Quoted in Rachel Walker, "Cotton Mather," Salem Witch Trials. www.iath.virginia.edu/salem/people/c_mather.html.
16. Quoted in Hill, *The Salem Witch Trials Reader,* p. 61.
17. Quoted in Roach, *The Salem Witch Trials,* p. 18.

Chapter Three: The First Accused Witches Are Questioned

18. Karlsen, *The Devil in the Shape of a Woman,* p. 45.
19. Starkey, *The Devil in Massachusetts,* p. 49.

20. Starkey, *The Devil in Massachusetts,* p. 51.
21. Starkey, *The Devil in Massachusetts,* p. 51.
22. Quoted in Roach, *The Salem Witch Trials,* p. 25.
23. Quoted in Roach, *The Salem Witch Trials,* p. 26.
24. Quoted in Roach, *The Salem Witch Trials,* p. 27.
25. Quoted in Roach, *The Salem Witch Trials,* p. 30.
26. Quoted in Roach, *The Salem Witch Trials,* p. 31.
27. Quoted in Hill, *The Salem Witch Trials Reader,* p. 62.
28. Quoted in Hill, *The Salem Witch Trials Reader,* p. 299.

Chapter Four: The Infamous Witch Trials Begin

29. Quoted in Hill, *The Salem Witch Trials Reader,* p. 102.
30. Quoted in Hill, *The Salem Witch Trials Reader,* p. 101.
31. Roach, *The Salem Witch Trials,* pp. 158–59.
32. Quoted in Chadwick Hansen, *Witchcraft at Salem.* New York: George Braziller, 1985, p. 65.
33. Quoted in George L. Burr, ed., *Narratives of the Witchcraft Cases, 1648–1706.* New York: Barnes and Noble, 1975, p. 352.
34. Roach, *The Salem Witch Trials,* p. 168.
35. Quoted in Hansen, *Witchcraft at Salem,* p. 126.
36. Quoted in Frances Hill, *A Delusion of Satan: The Full Story of the Salem Witch Trials.* New York: Da Capo, 2002, p. 156.

Chapter Five: Salem in the Grip of Mass Hysteria

37. Starkey, *The Devil in Massachusetts,* pp. 46–47.
38. Quoted in Hill, *The Salem Witch Trials Reader,* p. 77.
39. Quoted in Hill, *The Salem Witch Trials Reader,* pp. 77–78.
40. Quoted in Hill, *A Delusion of Satan,* p. 176.
41. Quoted in Starkey, *The Devil in Massachusetts,* p. 93.
42. Quoted in Starkey, *The Devil in Massachusetts,* p. 94.
43. Quoted in Starkey, *The Devil in Massachusetts,* p. 94.
44. Starkey, *The Devil in Massachusetts,* pp. 94–95.
45. Quoted in Electronic Text Center, University of Virginia Library, *The Salem Witchcraft Papers,* vol. 1, "Benjamin Abbot v. Martha Carrier." http://etext.virginia.edu/etcbin/toccernew2?id=BoySal1.sgm&images=images/modeng&data=/texts/english/modeng/oldsalem&tag=public&part=140&division=div2.
46. Quoted in Burr, *Narratives of the Witchcraft Cases,* p. 244.
47. Quoted in Roach, *The Salem Witch Trials,* p. 227.
48. Quoted in Hill, *The Salem Witch Trials Reader,* pp. 194–95.
49. Quoted in Roach, *The Salem Witch Trials,* p. 77.
50. Quoted in Roach, *The Salem Witch Trials,* p. 297.

Chapter Six: Too Many Witches: The Trials End

51. Quoted in Hill, *The Salem Witch Trials Reader,* p. 98.

52. Quoted in Burr, *Narratives of the Witchcraft Cases*, p. 201.
53. Starkey, *The Devil in Massachusetts*, p. 230.
54. Quoted in Starkey, *The Devil in Massachusetts*, p. 250.
55. Quoted in M.H. Thomas, ed., *The Diary of Samuel Sewall*. New York: Farrar, Straus, and Giroux, 1973, p. 97.
56. Quoted in Matthew Dennis, Department of History, University of Oregon, "Ann Putnam's Confession (1706)." www.uoregon.edu/~mjden nis/courses/wk3_putnam.htm.
57. Quoted in Roach, *The Salem Witch Trials*, p. 572.

Epilogue: The Popular Legacy of the Trials

58. Arthur Miller, "Why I Wrote 'The Crucible,'" *New Yorker*. www.new yorker.com/archive/content/?020 422fr_archive02.
59. Hill, *The Salem Witch Trials Reader*, p. xviii.

For Further Reading

Books

Tracey Boraas, *The Salem Witch Trials.* Mankato, MN: Capstone, 2003. An excellent introduction for young people to the weird and frightening trials of witches in Salem in the 1600s.

Paul Boyer and Stephen Nissenbaum, *Salem Possessed: The Social Origins of Witchcraft.* Cambridge, MA: Harvard University Press, 1974. Many historians consider this the most important recent study of the reasons for the witchcraft hysteria in Salem.

George L. Burr, ed., *Narratives of the Witchcraft Cases, 1648–1706.* New York: Barnes and Noble, 1975. One of the more complete collections of primary sources about the Salem witch trials.

Frances Hill, *A Delusion of Satan: The Full Story of the Salem Witch Trials.* New York: Da Capo, 2002. A well-organized and well-written account of the trials by one of the leading authorities on the subject.

———, ed., *The Salem Witch Trials Reader.* New York: Da Capo, 2000. A hefty collection of primary sources relating to the trials in Salem.

Laura Marvel, ed., *The Salem Witch Trials.* San Diego: Greenhaven, 2003. A useful collection of articles about the trials, couched in Greenhaven's renowned Opposing Viewpoints format.

Marilynne K. Roach, *The Salem Witch Trials: A Day-by-Day Chronicle of a Community Under Siege.* New York: Taylor Trade, 2002. This large (600+ pages), meticulously researched book goes into extraordinary detail describing every aspect of the Salem witch trials, including a great deal of primary source material.

Marion L. Starkey, *The Devil in Massachusetts: A Modern Enquiry into the Salem Witch Trials.* New York: Random House, 1989. One of the better general modern overviews of the witch trials in Salem.

Web Sites

Salem Massachusetts City Guide (www.salemweb.com/guide/witches.shtml). Provides an enlightening overview of the famous town, then and now, with several links to sites with further information about the town and the famous witch trials.

Salem Witchcraft Trials, 1692, Famous American Trials (www.law.umkc.edu/faculty/projects/ftrials/salem/salem.htm). One of noted scholar Douglas Linder's excellent overviews of famous trials, including numerous primary source documents.

Index

Picture Credits

Cover photo: The Granger Collection, New York. Reproduced by permission.
AP Images, 92
© Archivo Iconographico/S.A./Corbis, 8 (top)
© Bettmann/Corbis, 13, 20, 24-25, 36, 45, 63, 71
Jerry Cooke, Pix Inc./Time Life Pictures/Getty Images, 42, 50
© Corbis, 57, 70
Eliot Elisofon/Time Life Pictures/Getty Images, 21
Getty Images, 41, 59
The Granger Collection, New York. Reproduced by permission, 43, 52, 61, 73
© Thomas A. Heinz/Corbis, 78
Hulton Archive/Getty Images, 76
Nina Leen/Time Life Pictures/Getty Images, 12, 80
Library of Congress, 8 (lower left), 18, 55, 83, 91
Mansell/Time Life Pictures/Getty Images, 47
Mary Evans Picture Library. Reproduced by permission, 14, 17
MPI/Getty Images, 22
North Wind Picture Archives. Reproduced by permission, 33
The Picture Desk, Inc., 92
© Lee Snider/Corbis, 46, 65, 84
© Stapleton Collection/Corbis, 11, 35

About the Author

Historian and award-winning author Don Nardo has written many books for young people about American history, including *The American Revolution, The Mexican-American War, The Declaration of Independence,* several volumes on the history and culture of Native Americans, and biographies of presidents Thomas Jefferson, Andrew Johnson, and Franklin D. Roosevelt. Mr. Nardo lives with his wife, Christine, in Massachusetts.